THE PRISONER LIST

The Prisoner List

A true story of defeat, captivity and salvation
in the Far East: 1941-45

Richard Kandler

MARSWORTH

First published in the United Kingdom in 2010
by Marsworth Publishing.

ISBN 978-0-9564881-0-7

The front cover photograph shows
a jungle clearing in Thailand.

The back cover illustration shows
a detail from a drawing by Jack Chalker, from his book
Burma Railway: Images of War
(The Original War Drawings of Japanese POW Jack Chalker).

For Emma

'Prisoners cannot complain as they are lucky not to have been dead before.'

Japanese commandant's response
to request for improved conditions

Kinsayok, Thailand, 1943

CONTENTS

MAPS

Acknowledgements

THE VAST MAJORITY of this book was written more than
sixteen years ago, based almost entirely on a series of taped
conversations that I had had with my father eighteen months
before that.

The purpose of making the tapes had simply been to create a
permanent record of his recollection of certain events that he
rarely talked about. When I later had the idea of turning the
tapes into a book, I did not mention it to him and never showed
him what I had written. His strong inclination was always to live
in the present; having quizzed him for so many hours about the
past, I felt that I had troubled him more than enough.

Were it not for his patience and his clarity throughout those
conversations – and his willingness to answer whatever
questions I asked him, no matter how inane – this book could
never have been written.

I have also received help from a number of other sources.

Jean Roberts has provided me with an invaluable mine of
information compiled by herself and Frank Clark, regarding the
men and experiences of Saigon Battalion; Jean's own father was
one of the two men punished for taking biscuits from the Saigon
docks, as described towards the end of Chapter 17. Alan Wills,
whose father survived the sinking of the *Kachidoki Maru*, has
supplied me with further material which I have also used.

I am grateful to Yvonne Huntriss for her kind permission to
quote from the war diaries (held at the Imperial War Museum)
of her late brother Lieutenant Louis Baume, whom my father
knew. The passage that I have quoted was drawn to my attention
by Brian MacArthur, through the pages of his outstanding book
Surviving the Sword (published by Time Warner Books).

The illustration on the back cover is a detail from one of a large collection of drawings by Jack Chalker, from the time when he too was a prisoner of war; he and Louis Baume were among those who took enormous risks to record their experiences for posterity. The complete drawing, and a great many of his others, can be found in Mr Chalker's remarkably effective book *Burma Railway: Images of War* (published by Mercer Books), which also sets out his own vivid recollections.

I am therefore indebted to Mr Chalker for agreeing to my use of this illustration, and to Tim Mercer of Mercer Books for contacting him on my behalf.

Miles Bailey of The Choir Press has guided me painlessly through the publishing process. Thanks are also due to Harriet Evans for her meticulous proofreading (which was even more scrupulous than the text and layout of this final version might suggest) and to Martin Field for his excellent presentational thoughts and ideas.

My mother and sister, Hilda and Rosalind, have known about this book and yet resisted the urge to suggest – let alone insist – that I show them a draft that they could vet or comment upon. That is an act of considerable forbearance, and one which I hope they will not regret.

My wife Emma has been saddled with the opposite problem: I have burdened her with the book far too much and run almost every chapter past her. She has been hugely supportive and made some invaluable suggestions which I have taken on board.

She and our children – Louise and Tom Kandler – have been extremely patient in recent months, during which this book has encroached on more of our home life than I had intended that it would. My thanks also go to Louise for her help with the maps and to Tom for his thoughts on the book cover.

Richard Kandler
London
31 March 2010

Preface

THIS BOOK is the result of a series of taped conversations that I had with my father when he was seventy-five.

He rarely mentioned his years as a prisoner of war in the Far East, and was not at all keen on the idea of being interviewed in this way when I first suggested it to him. However he eventually agreed to it and, once we had started, he began to speak much more openly to me than ever before about what had happened.

As a result, I have been able to tell much of the story more or less in his own words; these are the areas shown in speech marks and italics. I say 'more or less', because I have made some adjustments to his original wording in order to ease the flow of the narrative. *The substance remains unchanged.*

Pseudonyms

His name was Reuben Kandler, but throughout the book I call him Ben – a name by which he was never known to anybody. I briefly say in the first chapter why I have done this.

I have also changed some of the other characters' names; these are the ones marked with an asterisk in the index. Where I have given somebody a pseudonym, it is normally because (for one reason or another) it felt wrong to me to use the person's actual name without his or her family's permission. Seeking that permission would in most cases be impractical, and would also risk reawakening painful memories for those concerned.

There have been other reasons too for using pseudonyms. For example, there are a number of instances where I have been unable to track down the correct spelling of a person's surname. In these cases I have preferred to use a false name that I could spell (illogical though I know that is).

Siam/Thailand

Siam's name was changed to Thailand shortly before the Second World War, and then back to Siam when the war was over. Four years later, it was changed to Thailand again – this time for good.

So, during the events described in this book, the country's formal name was Thailand. I have therefore used that name even though most people at the time – including the prisoners of war who were being held there – still tended to think of it as Siam.

Choice of words

With very few exceptions, I have stuck to normal everyday language rather than use some of the Japanese, regional or army terms that the prisoners would have used at the time. So I say 'rest days' instead of *'yasume* days*'*, 'stretchers' instead of *'tongas'*, and 'warehouses' instead of *'godowns'*.

More particularly, I say 'camp shop' instead of 'canteen'. I do not especially like the expression 'camp shop', but the image that most people (including me) associate with the word 'canteen' – as being some basic form of restaurant – is so far removed from the facts that I have preferred not to use it.

Military rank

Francis Hugonin, Harold Lilly and Alfred 'Knocker' Knights were lieutenant-colonels (not full colonels). In spite of that, I have referred to them simply as colonels, as that is what they were usually called in conversation. I have adopted the same principle in relation to Arthur Percival, who was a lieutenant-general.

(None of these are pseudonyms, by the way.)

The Japanese held the Allies' highest-ranking officers, from full colonels upwards, separately from the other ranks; there would not normally have been a prisoner above the rank of lieutenant-colonel in any of the camps where this book is set.

The 'Hanoi Hundred'

There is one area where I have simplified the facts, as they complicate the story without (in my opinion) adding much. For completeness, I shall set out the full position here.

I have said in the book that a thousand prisoners were shipped from Singapore to Saigon, including two doctors; the actual numbers were 1,118 prisoners (joined by five more soon after), including three doctors (not two). On reaching Saigon, however, about a hundred of these men, accompanied by one of the three doctors, were sent to Hanoi to build an airstrip. This left just over a thousand prisoners, including two doctors, at Saigon.

The 'Hanoi Hundred' did not return to Saigon until November 1942. Of these, only the doctor was among the seven hundred prisoners moved from Saigon to Thailand in June 1943.

The 'prisoner list' that was later compiled in Thailand could not include these one hundred men, as the sergeant-majors who held their details had remained with them in Saigon. The list did however cover all the other prisoners – over a thousand in total.

Scope

This book is not supposed to be exhaustive: Colonel Hugonin's immense personal courage went far beyond the incidents that I have described, and Basil Bancroft was not the only prisoner who broke out of the Saigon camp for food and medicines. Similarly, Tom Cobham and Adam Stock (as I have called them) were not the only men who – for one purpose or another – crossed the ditch at Tamuang.

Part title pages

I have taken some liberties with the wording of the passages shown as quotations on the title pages for Parts 3, 4 and 5. I have done this only to assist the overall tone of the book; the mood and message of the original wording remains the same.

Friends

The book says relatively little about the friendships and sense of community that existed among the prisoners. Perhaps I could go some small way towards remedying that (using actual names, not pseudonyms) here.

Jack Bunston is mentioned only briefly, but he was with my father throughout. He slept on the bunk bed above him on the way out to Singapore, quickly becoming an invaluable friend and remaining so for the whole of their captivity – particularly when my father had malaria. They remained friends until Jack's early death some years after the war.

Just after reaching Saigon, when Jack Bunston and my father had dysentery, two men who were then complete strangers to them – Jock Bremner and Jimmy Rennie – gave them their first pay from the docks to enable them to purchase food from the camp shop. Another, Jim Spencer, gave them some sardines that he had stolen from the docks. This quickly became a pattern of behaviour that continued throughout the men's captivity.

Later, on the railway, this kind of comradeship became even more important. My father owed much, for example, to John Berry, who would take the pressure off him when it came to the hammer-and-tap work – a job my father simply could not do.

But these are only snapshots. There was more to this than isolated acts of selflessness: it was a way of life and a survival system.

♦

Finally, for those wanting to read more about the building of the railway, I have appended (from page 207) my father's own description of that ordeal. He wrote it while he was still a prisoner of war, having been ordered to produce an account of his experiences for the Japanese propaganda machine.

It was written only a few months after the completion of the railway – with the death toll still rising.

Part One

Into the Unknown

'*Human history advances with bleeding feet.*'

Chinese merchant on the River Kwai

– 1 –
Before Leaving

His BIG CHANCE came on day five.

He was called away from the parade ground during basic training and told that he was wanted in the barracks office.

The young orderly who had been sent to fetch him led the way and showed him into a room where a captain and a lieutenant were seated at a table. They invited him to sit down. Then they explained. They had two thousand men at the barracks and two thousand more about to arrive. The barracks' pay system could not cope with those numbers and was in chaos. They needed somebody to run the payroll full-time – and their records showed that he was a chartered accountant.

It was perfect: his first stripe straight away, a second stripe after the first six weeks, an entire war spent overseeing the pay system at Arborfield Barracks, and the ability to be home within an hour whenever he had leave. But he blew it:

'I asked them if this was an order or a request. It was a request, and so I declined.

I'd been certified as A1 fit and had opted to go into the Royal Artillery expecting to fight. The job they were describing didn't really require my accountancy knowledge and I didn't see how I could justify spending the war in the barracks office operating the payroll.'

The two officers said they understood his reasons and wished him luck as he went back to his rifle practice.

He could never have dreamt what lay ahead.

He had been born twenty-five years earlier into a large observant Jewish household on 30 or 31 March (nobody knew which) 1916.

His parents lived in the same street as his grandparents, uncles and aunts in the East End of London. His father made clothes for a living, from a workshop at the back of their house.

School began on his fifth birthday. He was not supposed to have started that day (the end of March being close to the end of term), but his parents had told him that he would begin when he was five and he had taken them too literally; when his birthday came, he was so insistent on going to school that his mother took him in anyway. The teachers agreed to have him for what was left of the term, and put him up a year when he returned at the end of the holidays.

He was moved up another year shortly afterwards, and then again after that, until he was being taught in a class of children much older than him. He went on to win a scholarship to a prominent boys' school in central London, where his strongest subjects were maths and sciences and he achieved the school's best ever physics results. But university was not a feasible option; instead of staying on at school with a view to a physics degree, he left to train as a chartered accountant.

I have decided to call him Ben. I am reluctant to refer to him by his actual first name – Reuben – as nobody of my age ever called him that. Shortening Reuben to Ben (a name by which he was never known to anybody) seems to sidestep that problem.

♦

Ben left school in the depths of the Great Depression. Money and jobs were scarce, and political extremism was on the rise.

Hitler was gaining ground in Germany, and a new right-wing political party had been launched at home. The British Union of Fascists held rabble-rousing rallies on an increasingly anti-Semitic platform and sought to stage provocative uniformed marches through the Jewish areas of London's East End. For families like Ben's, the fascists became impossible to ignore.

But life went on, and in 1938 Ben qualified as a chartered accountant. He was placed first out of six hundred candidates – not just overall, but in every single paper except one. He won the First Certificate of Merit, the Institute Prize, the W.B. Peat Gold Medal and Prize, and the William Quilter Prize.

There was not much else to celebrate. Since coming to power in Germany, Hitler had embarked on a massive rearmaments programme; he spoke openly of German expansionism, and now his ruthless brand of militarist fascism was threatening to engulf Europe. The month after Ben qualified, Hitler annexed Austria.

Six months later, it was Czechoslovakia's turn to be invaded.

The following winter brought more bad news of a different kind, when Ben's father died unexpectedly after a short illness. Ben's mother, although she did not yet know it, would have to endure every parent's worst nightmares on her own.

◆

Her first son to leave was Harry – Ben's brother.

Harry was in the Territorial Army. He was called up for active service on 1 September 1939, the day that Hitler invaded Poland. Two days later, Britain and Germany were at war.

Britain had prepared for the worst: air raid shelters, gas masks, and blackout material for night-time bombing raids. Ben was summoned to an army depot to retrieve his younger brother Sam, who had run away from school to join up and fight the Nazis; but the war itself, in the early months, was uneventful.

That changed in the spring, when Germany launched invasions into Denmark and Norway – followed by Belgium, Holland, Luxembourg and France. By June 1940, Hitler's grip on Europe extended all the way to the English Channel.

In September, the Blitz began: sustained aerial bombing over British towns and cities, with London as the prime target.

Ben and his family moved out to Edgware, on London's northern outskirts. The workshop at the back of their old house – the one that his late father had worked from – was bombed soon afterwards.

Then news arrived of Ben's brother Harry: he had been captured by Rommel's troops in North Africa.

Matters could very easily have been worse. Hitler had ordered the annihilation of all Jewish prisoners of war, but Rommel – no enthusiast for Nazi policies – had disobeyed.

Harry's group had been handed over to the Italians. They were holding him in central Italy, in accordance with the terms of the Geneva Convention.

♦

By now, Ben had started his basic military training at Arborfield Barracks. I say 'started', because he never finished. Shortly after turning down the payroll job, he and selected others were transferred to separate barracks for training of an entirely different kind.

It was top secret: a new and rapidly developing technology, in which Britain was well ahead of the rest of the world and which was seen as crucial to the success of the war. It went under the name of 'radio location', but it was soon to acquire the label by which it is known today: radar.

Radar was in its infancy, but it was already capable of many different uses.

At Devonport in Plymouth, Ben was trained in coastal radar, which could track the movement of enemy ships. At the end of the course, Ben achieved the highest marks in the class and was selected for the 'No. 1' course – so called because its purpose was to train candidates to act in the lead (or 'No. 1') role in a unit of, typically, four radar operators.

Ben passed the No. 1 examination, which earned him his first stripe. He was now one rank up from a gunner: a lance-bombardier.

More importantly, Ben had scored the highest marks out of all the No. 1 examination candidates. On the strength of this, he was recommended to the War Office for a highly coveted place on the 'technical instructors' – or 'TI' – radar course.

'*The TI course covered everything that there was to know about radar, and carried an immediate promotion to the rank of sergeant-major for those who successfully completed it.*'

For Ben, however, it might well lead to more than that. He had applied for a place on the Officer Cadet Training Unit; were he to become an officer, completion of the TI course would automatically bring him to the rank of major.

'*But I couldn't begin the TI course until I'd had a very thorough security vetting by the War Office. Radar was top secret and they couldn't take any risks.*
So I had to wait for my War Office interview first.'

No specific date for the interview had been set, but he knew that it would not be for several weeks. Meanwhile, he was to remain at Devonport until he was summoned to the War Office.

◆

The Jewish New Year was looming. The War Office interview would not be taking place until some time after that, and so Ben applied for leave to spend the two-day festival with his family.

It was not easy obtaining permission, but Ben pressed the point:

'*I was only on standby at Devonport, waiting for my War Office interview – my absence for two days couldn't make any difference to the war effort.*
It was better for me to take leave now than later.'

Ben was eventually granted his two days, and travelled home to Edgware in late September 1941.

It was only to be a short visit, but the memory of it would remain firmly in his mind over the years that lay ahead: he would not see his family again until after the end of the war.

As the second day drew to a close, the time came for Ben to return to Devonport and he was soon on the late train back to Plymouth.

Ben arrived at the barracks during the night, and reported in at the guardroom:

'While they were checking me in, one of them said that my name had been put down to go overseas within the next few days. Complete surprise to me.

Later that morning I found out it was true. There'd been a change of plan.

A No. 1 radar operator I knew called Gridley, who'd been due to go overseas, had gone sick. I'd been selected to take his place.

I never saw Gridley again after that.'

There would be no War Office interview, no TI course, and no place on the Officer Cadet Training Unit.

Nor was there time to measure Ben up for a uniform, and so he was given Gridley's. It was much too large for Ben; it was also made out of noticeably thinner material than Ben's existing uniform, suggesting a hot climate:

'They couldn't tell me where I was being posted to. They probably didn't know themselves – or not officially.

But there were a couple of old sweats standing around who recognised the uniform I'd been given and who seemed to know what it meant. One of them wandered over to me and whispered in my ear: "You're going to Singapore."'

A distant war was brewing – and it was not the one that Ben thought he had been called up to fight.

He would be sailing from Liverpool in five days' time.

The Dominion Monarch

THE *Dominion Monarch* sailed north out of Liverpool, west along the northern coast of Scotland, and south into the Atlantic in a convoy of twenty-five ships. To avoid enemy submarines, they sailed down to the southern tip of Africa and then east.

It was worlds away from anything Ben had ever experienced: crossing the equator, the electrical storms in the south Atlantic, the tiny bumboats off the coast of Sierra Leone, and the five days spent in Cape Town. After that the convoy thinned out, and the ships went their different ways.

Those on the *Dominion Monarch* headed eastwards, where they saw flying fish in the Indian Ocean and stopped for a brief stay in Ceylon (now Sri Lanka). Then they continued east.

♦

None of the men had officially been told their destination and, strictly speaking, they were not supposed to know. Yet many of them had suspected from the uniforms that they were going to the Far East; as they sailed across the Indian Ocean, Singapore looked increasingly likely.

But why Singapore?

'We weren't given a specific reason. Singapore was a British colony then, but there was no war going on there – not yet.

We knew the Japanese were causing trouble in other parts of the Far East, but we weren't at war with them. With Hitler overrunning Europe and bombing our cities, whatever was happening in Asia seemed very distant to us.'

It was only three years earlier that a British prime minister had spoken of 'a quarrel in a far-away country between people of whom we know nothing'. He had not been referring to the Far East, but to events in central Europe – yet it had not seemed such a ludicrous remark at the time: few people had ever flown, overseas travel was slow, and foreign holidays for most were unaffordable. Many of those on the *Dominion Monarch* – including Ben – had never been abroad until now.

So to be shipped to the Far East, at short notice and with no real explanation, was a formidable plunge into the unknown; it was entirely unexpected – especially for Ben, for whom there had been no hint of an overseas posting until five days earlier. The men on the *Dominion Monarch* thought they had been called up to fight against Germany: not to protect far-flung colonies from a possible threat posed by Japan.

'With everything that had been happening on our doorstep, we had only a vague idea of what had been going on in Asia.

But what most of us did know – because the details had been so very shocking – was that the Japanese had invaded China before the outbreak of war and committed the most horrible atrocities. It had become known as the "Rape of Nanking".'

Nanking had, at the time, been China's capital city. Tens of thousands of Chinese women and girls had been savagely raped, and an even greater number of men and boys brutally tortured and butchered to death, in six weeks of orchestrated barbarity.

The aim had been to force the Chinese there into submission. Depressingly, it had succeeded.

'So we knew the Japanese were in China. But what most of us hadn't realised, because it had been overshadowed for us by events in Europe, was that French Indo-China was no longer French. The Japanese were there too and were running the place.

We found that out for ourselves later on.'

There had been no specific threat of an attack on Singapore, but clearly the authorities were becoming nervous.

♦

Singapore was an island at the foot of Malaya, a loose collection of British colonies and protected states on the Malay Peninsula.

Malaya was the world's largest producer of tin and rubber, making the area hugely valuable to Britain – and so also, potentially, to Japan:

'It was feared – correctly, as matters turned out – that the Japanese wanted those natural resources to help fund their continuing war in the Pacific.

But, as we later discovered, they had a separate purpose for wanting to occupy Singapore too.'

It was a particularly sinister purpose: to exterminate those elements of Singapore's large Chinese population who were providing financial aid to China.

The Japanese also saw Singapore as a strategic launch pad for more invasions:

'They wanted power. They wanted to spread themselves all over South-East Asia and dominate that part of the world.

And they very nearly succeeded.'

♦

It was during his nine weeks on the *Dominion Monarch* that Ben was first introduced to someone whose name will feature throughout this book: Second Lieutenant Youle.

Second Lieutenant Youle

SECOND LIEUTENANT YOULE was from Edgware, where Ben's family had moved at the start of the Blitz.

Both he and Ben were known to the ship's physical training instructor, who introduced them to each other when he learned that they were both from the same area.

Before being called up, Youle had been living at home with his mother.

After meeting Ben, he wrote to her and said in his letter that there was someone else on board who was also from Edgware.

He mentioned Ben by name.

♦

When Mrs Youle received the letter, she found out where Ben's mother lived and went to visit her.

The two mothers kept in close contact – as Ben would discover on his return home in four years' time.

Part Two

The Naked Island

'I confess that in my mind the whole Japanese
menace lay in a sinister twilight, compared with our
other needs.'

Winston S. Churchill
The Grand Alliance, 1950

– 4 –
Changi

SINGAPORE ISLAND was similar in shape to the Isle of Wight, but slightly larger – and much, much hotter. The sweltering humidity of the tropics bore down on the new arrivals from Britain, as they disembarked in the oppressive heat and waited for instructions.

After a long day of confusion and uncertainty, Ben's radar group finally received their orders and boarded a truck for Changi Barracks. There they would be attached to a British heavy anti-aircraft regiment of regular army personnel, permanently stationed at Singapore.

The regiment had a radar set, but had not until now had anyone who knew what to do with it.

◆

Changi was on the eastern tip of the island:

'They were very fine barracks. First class. All mod cons.'

Those were his exact words to me about Changi Barracks. There was no hint of sarcasm in his voice or of deliberate exaggeration.

'They were new barracks and the buildings were excellent. So were all the amenities.
There was a Chinese seamstress who would come in and, if we wanted anything done to our uniforms, we just waited for Sew-Sew – that was what we called her – and she'd do it for us.'

Sew-Sew adjusted Ben's uniform, which was too large for him, having been intended for Gridley.

Some more unusual services were provided too:

'There were barbers – they were Chinese, not Malayan. They'd come into the barracks at night, while we were asleep under our mosquito nets. Very lax security arrangements when you think about it.

Anyway, we'd be fast asleep and the barbers would be in the room with us, moving from bed to bed. During the night, they'd pull up each of our mosquito nets, lather us up and then shave us while we slept.'

Changi Barracks would have been even more luxurious if Chinese athletes had come in each day to do all the regiment's fitness training for them.

The men were woken at five each morning, so that they could start before the worst of the heat set in. (If they had had to shave themselves they would have needed to get up even earlier, and so there was a purpose served by the night-time barbers.)

The day began with a forty-five minute run, followed by a shower. After that the men ate their breakfast in the dining hall before going on parade. The rest of the day was spent on the same drills and routines that Ben had been introduced to at Arborfield Barracks: rifle training, bayonet practice, square-bashing, running, and seemingly endless fitness routines.

For Ben it was like a resumption of his basic training, but now in an unbearably hot climate where the air humidity felt almost tangible. The drill sergeants pushed the newcomers from Britain relentlessly, through the blistering heat of the long tropical day. The clammy atmosphere clung to them and weighed down their every move; everything here was an effort.

The sheer exertion of it all raised an unsettling question, particularly in the minds of those like Ben who had just arrived: How would they cope in these temperatures in a real life combat situation, against a strong and determined enemy?

Many of the recruits were too exhausted to give the question much thought, or simply preferred to close their eyes to it. Others tried to reassure themselves by believing outmoded colonial nonsense: that Japanese fighters were short-sighted and puny, with no sense of balance and unable to see in the dark.

Yet the men knew they had been posted here for a reason, and this was particularly true of the regular soldiers who had been on the island for some time. After months of preparation, the regulars had grown accustomed to living perpetually on standby – for an attack that might or might not happen.

Ben, however, never reached that stage. It was during only his tenth night on the island that his war started in earnest:

'We were woken in the small hours by a sound that I hadn't heard since we'd left home. It was an air raid siren.'

I do not know whether it was before or after Ben had had his visit from the barber. It probably no longer matters.

'Some of the regular soldiers were surprisingly unconcerned about it and just wanted to go back to sleep. There'd been so many practice drills before our arrival that they thought this was just another one.

But, for those of us who'd been in London during the Blitz, it was impossible to ignore. So we ran out onto the nearest balcony to see what was going on.'

That was another impressive feature of Changi Barracks: balconies all along each floor.

'From there, we saw anti-aircraft shells bursting in the sky. This wasn't just a drill. The Japanese were bombing Singapore.'

It was 8 December 1941. Across the international date line, they were doing the same to Pearl Harbor.

The Impregnable Fortress

SINGAPORE owed her reputation as an impregnable fortress to two main factors: the huge coastal guns and the magnificent new Naval Base.

The coastal guns pointed out towards the Pacific, and were mainly of use against sea invasion.[1] Their chief purpose was to protect the Naval Base, at the north.

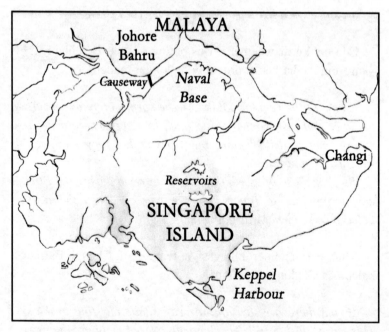

---

[1] Some of them could be turned inwards or towards the north, but they were not equipped with the right ammunition for firing at invading ground troops.

The Naval Base covered a colossal twenty-one square miles, and was the most advanced construction of its kind anywhere in the world. It had taken twenty years to build at a cost of more than sixty million pounds (equivalent to £2.5 billion in 2006) and had been designed to house a vast fleet of ships that would protect Britain's interests in South-East Asia.

All that was needed now was the vast fleet of ships – or any ships at all. The Naval Base was the cornerstone of British defence policy in the region; yet it had stood practically vacant from the time of its opening four years earlier.

It was still empty when Ben arrived on the island at the end of November 1941.

But four days later, to immense relief, that changed.

On 2 December 1941, a fleet dominated by the formidable HMS *Prince of Wales* and HMS *Repulse* arrived from Britain. They were two of the world's mightiest warships, and far superior to anything in the Japanese fleet.

Churchill had announced that they were being sent to the Far East as a clear show of strength. He had also written to tell President Roosevelt – whom he had secretly met on the *Prince of Wales* four months earlier – where the great ship was going:

> This ought to serve as a deterrent on Japan. There is nothing like having something that can catch and kill anything.

With war raging in Europe, few had expected any ships to be provided – even in the event of an attack.

Now at long last the Naval Base had its fleet. The *Prince of Wales* and the *Repulse* would be Singapore's salvation.

♦

There was little else to depend on:

> '*Britain scarcely had enough resources to defend itself again Nazi Germany, let alone to send out to distant colonies.*'

So the Allies in the region (British, Indian, Australian and
Malay) had no tanks, while the Japanese had two hundred – but
the position in the air was even worse.

The few aircraft available to the Allies were small, slow,
unreliable and obsolete: they were barely worth having. The
Japanese had hundreds of state-of-the-art heavy bombers; the
Allies had none.

◆

Five nights after the high profile arrival of the *Prince of Wales*
and the *Repulse*, the Japanese launched their night-time bombing
raid on Singapore.

The bombers were gone by morning.

The raid had been a diversionary tactic: shortly after
midnight, Japanese forces had landed on the coast of northern
Malaya. They had reached the Malay Peninsula by sea from
French Indo-China (already under Japanese influence).

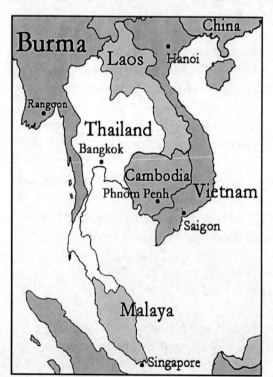

*French
Indo-China
comprised
Vietnam,
Cambodia
and Laos.*

The invincible HMS *Prince of Wales* and HMS *Repulse* set out from the Naval Base and headed north to intercept further Japanese landings. They sailed without air cover.

After they had made some headway, bomber aircraft struck. The two ships were destroyed in the early afternoon.

No ship of their stature had ever been sunk by air attack. But now – just two days into the campaign – it had happened to both of them in the space of an hour.

◆

Ben was in the dining hall at Changi Barracks when the news came through on the radio:

'We couldn't believe what we were hearing. It was unimaginable that ships of that kind could have been sunk with so little apparent difficulty. An order was immediately issued to disregard what we'd heard: it just couldn't be true.

But later on it was confirmed that it really had happened. You can imagine the effect on morale – we'd placed so much hope on those ships.

It was a major disaster, right at the start of the campaign.

Not only did we have no tanks and no air force to speak of: we had no navy either.'

◆

Churchill was shaken too.

He was in bed when the First Sea Lord, Sir Dudley Pound, telephoned him with the news. He later wrote:

In all the war I never received a more direct shock ... As I turned over and twisted in bed the full horror of the news sank in upon me. There were no British or American ships in the Indian Ocean or the Pacific except the American survivors of Pearl Harbor, who were hastening back to California. Over all this vast expanse of waters Japan was supreme, and we everywhere were weak and naked.

6

The Naval Base

EVEN WITH THE FLEET SUNK, the Naval Base was strategically vital.

The defence of Malaya and Singapore now depended on the early arrival of reinforcements by sea: their safe passage and disembarkation would be jeopardised unless the Naval Base remained intact and under Allied control.

So Ben's radar team were ordered to take up posts in southern Malaya. There they would be well positioned to anticipate threats from the air to the all-important Naval Base.

♦

They boarded trucks which headed north across the Causeway, the bridge linking Singapore to the mainland. There they were stationed in a rubber plantation at the south of the Malay Peninsula, just to the north of Johore Bahru.[2]

The radar equipment was set up among the rubber trees, alongside two heavy artillery guns. The climate was the same as it had been on the island: very hot and very muggy.

The radar machinery was made up of three separate parts.

The first of these was a diesel engine, to generate the power.

The second was a transmitting cabin, with a vast rotating aerial over it. The aerial sent out an electronic signal to locate enemy aircraft. If any information was detected, it was picked up by a separate receiving cabin; that was the third part.

---

[2] The map on page 18 shows where this is.

The receiving cabin was manned by four operators (in contrast to the transmitting cabin, which was automated and so did not require constant attention). Three of the operators monitored their separate radar screens, while the fourth – the 'No.1' operator – collated and co-ordinated their findings, and also diagnosed the causes of any difficulties that might arise with the equipment. Ben worked as the No.1 operator while he was on duty.

The two heavy guns, each manned by a team of eight or nine men, were nearby. They and the massive radar aerial were partially concealed by the rubber trees, but not entirely.

◆

'We'd see the local rubber-tappers turn up at the plantation first thing each morning.

They used a special knife to shave off a thin sliver of the bark of the rubber tree, and fitted a metal cup underneath which they wired around the trunk. Afterwards a white sap would trickle out into the cup. They'd collect it the next day to be processed.'

I have no idea whether the rubber-tappers took an equal interest in Ben and his radar equipment, although I cannot imagine what they would have made of it all if they had. It certainly sounded complicated when he explained it to me.

The receiving cabin would pick up information on approaching aircraft and translate it into a nine-digit number which incorporated all the particulars that the guns needed in order to know where to fire. The nine-digit number would be transmitted electronically to the two guns as soon as it was known. They also had a direct telephone link to Fort Canning – the military headquarters back on the island – and so the nine-digit number had to be telephoned through to Fort Canning too.

Consequently the radar group were relaying this information both to the two nearby guns and to Fort Canning, whenever they picked up signs of an oncoming raid.

The radar operators were generally on duty in eight-hour shifts, but even when they were off duty they stayed in the area. They slept, if they could, in a nearby tent:

'It wasn't constant action at first – not in the initial stages. Even when we were on duty, there'd be quiet periods when not much happened.

But then we'd pick up a raid and have to move very, very fast so that the guns could fire in time. The Japanese planes came over in convoys of 27, 54 and 108, and they'd all drop their bombs simultaneously – so there was never any time to lose.

We could pick up movements twenty miles off, which was remarkable – or at least it was in those days.'

♦

The early loss of the *Prince of Wales* and the *Repulse* had enabled thousands of Japanese to land in northern Malaya unopposed. Now they were advancing south.

Allied ground forces were sent up-country into the jungle to confront them. So were the guns:

'The two heavy guns that we'd been with were ordered to relocate further up the peninsula, so that they could intercept aircraft attacks in the north.

But we were to stay put in the rubber plantation.'

The radar group were still needed at the southern end of the peninsula, where they could continue to alert Fort Canning of oncoming threats to Singapore's Naval Base.

It may no longer have had any ships, but the security of the Naval Base remained paramount.

'Before the two guns were moved up north, mock-ups of them were built out of tree trunks.

When the guns had left, the mock-ups were placed in positions which made it look as if they were still there.'

The aim was to mislead any locals – more likely to be Malay than Chinese – who might covertly have been passing information to the other side.

◆

The air raids became progressively more frequent over the weeks that followed.

The radar operators were picking up many more signals than they had at the beginning, and there was another change too: now that the guns were gone, they were relaying their nine-digit numbers only to the headquarters at Fort Canning.

Although the two guns had left the rubber plantation, Fort Canning had direct contact with the fixed coastal artillery at Changi which covered the approaches to the Naval Base.

The system worked – but not always. As the weeks went on, and the bombings intensified, instances started to arise of Fort Canning failing to act on information provided by the radar unit. The reasons were never explained.

It could easily have proved disastrous, but no material damage was inflicted on the Naval Base.

◆

Further north, the men sent up-country were facing ferocious opposition.

The thousands of Japanese who had amassed there were rapidly heading south. They used light tank armaments to move quickly over the uneven terrain; the Allies did not have a single tank between them.

In the thick forests that covered much of the mainland, the attacking forces employed a ruthlessly aggressive form of jungle warfare for which they were thoroughly trained and well practised. Most of the defending troops had little or no combat experience; many had not even had time to acclimatise themselves to the gruelling climate and tropical conditions. The onslaught was relentless for them, and growing numbers were being pushed to exhaustion.

Hordes of Japanese fighters came down the peninsula on bicycles. They used them to move quietly, quickly and unpredictably so as to surprise and confuse. The speed and flexibility of the bicycles enabled them to get behind the Allied recruits and encircle them, cutting off any escape route.

The invaders climbed up trees and sniped down from above. They ambushed struggling foot soldiers in dense jungle areas, confronting them where they least expected it and forcing them into hand-to-hand combat.

The conduct of the Japanese troops crossed the line into barbarism – including against civilians.

In Penang, to the north, seven hundred local Chinese had been butchered and beheaded. In other areas, trapped Allied infantry were being tied up with barbed wire and used for bayonet practice.

'Word started getting to us of the most unspeakable massacres occurring in the jungle. Acts of breathtaking, wholly gratuitous savagery.'

As the enemy came closer, these atrocities began to move further south. In a village not far from the rubber plantation where Ben was stationed, scores of wounded Australian and Indian troops were being drowned, bayoneted and burned alive.

◆

Churchill knew of the enemy's swift assault down the peninsula.

He had also belatedly been advised of the true state of the defences of the supposed 'impregnable fortress' that lay at the foot of it. Now he feared for Singapore:

> I saw before me the hideous spectacle of the almost naked island and of the wearied, if not exhausted, troops retreating upon it.

It would soon be more than just a spectacle.

7

Mastery of the Skies

UNDER NO CIRCUMSTANCES could the Japanese be permitted to discover the secrets of radar. Not only would that endanger the Far East: it could jeopardise the war in Europe too.

Japan, Germany and Italy had signed a pact to stand together and support each other in the establishment of a new world order. Japan's war had nothing to do with Hitler's, but the possibility of Japan learning anything useful that might be passed to Germany had to be avoided at all costs.

So there were no radar sets north of Ben's unit: the diesel engine, the cabins and the huge aerial had to be kept well away from the invading Japanese ground troops, for fear that the enemy would find them and interrogate the radar operators.

By late January 1942, Fort Canning knew that the approaching Japanese forces could reach the rubber plantation – and the radar unit – at any time.

The radar team were ordered to leave Malaya and return to Singapore, with the radar set, immediately. They were driven by truck along the Causeway that day and stationed at the north of the island, still guarding the Naval Base.

Soon they were relocated again – this time, away from the Naval Base.

The Naval Base was no longer considered worth protecting – the opposite, in fact. The Japanese were surging towards it, and the whole area was set for imminent capture. It was too valuable to be allowed to fall into enemy hands, and so the Allied commanders – with Churchill's endorsement – resorted to a scorched earth policy: army demolition experts proceeded to wreck the fuel tanks, power station, cranes and workshops.

As much as possible of the empty Naval Base – the sixty million pound cornerstone of Britain's defence strategy in the Far East – was destroyed.

◆

The radar team were moved south, to the centre of the island.

They had a new purpose now: to protect the reservoirs.

'The reservoirs were a vital lifeline for Singapore, and so it was an important job for us – but not an easy one.

The Japanese had complete freedom of the skies, and they were making the most of it. The raids had grown more frequent as time had gone on, and we had a real sense now of being under siege. The situation was worse than ever.'

He paused for a moment. When he resumed, his tone was more reflective:

'I remember an afternoon when a few of us were off duty.

We sat on the wall around one of the reservoirs, each of us holding a bamboo stick with some string attached to it and a bent pin on the end of the string. Just casually fishing in the reservoir, with these rods that we'd put together.

There was chaos everywhere – more air raids, and the mounting feeling that the enemy were closing in. But we were off duty now and, whatever was going to happen next, we couldn't let circumstances get the better of us.

I don't think we caught any fish.'

◆

More Allied forces were returning across the Causeway. The Japanese on the mainland were now unstoppable; their hold on the peninsula was almost complete.

The Allied commanders had ordered a total withdrawal of troops from the Malay Peninsula back to the island. By the end of January, the last of the remaining Allied forces had returned.

The Malayan end of the Causeway was blown up by mines laid by the Allied engineers before leaving, so as at least to delay the Japanese arrival on Singapore.

Now there was only the island left. The Battle of Malaya had been lost.

◆

Ben's group were moved again – this time, to their final site: the Anson Road football stadium, which backed onto Keppel Harbour at the far south of the island.

The radar unit's purpose now was to protect the harbour and keep the sea lanes open for civilian evacuees heading for safety.[3]

The evacuation of women in particular – even nurses – had been dramatically accelerated, in the light of shocking news emerging from Hong Kong: first-hand reports of mass rapes being inflicted by the occupying forces on the local population. Hong Kong had fallen to the Japanese on Christmas Day.

A pattern had emerged.

Since their first posting on the peninsula, the radar unit had been drawn progressively further south to safeguard their top-secret equipment and technical expertise from enemy capture. Now they were at the very southern tip of the island.

They had spent most of the campaign defending the vast Naval Base on which everything had depended, for the arrival of reinforcements. Now, with the Naval Base abandoned, they were protecting the safe passage of civilians forced to flee.

◆

---

[3] The evacuees were mainly Europeans. The reason given was that finding a country which would accept non-Europeans was harder, as there were no sailings to China and ships to India were small and infrequent. Eventually Australia agreed to take 1,500 Chinese; others were sent to Ceylon.

The two heavy anti-aircraft guns and their operators had also returned from the peninsula. They were working alongside the radar unit again, as they had been in the Malayan rubber plantation at the start.

But now everything was closer-knit and the two large guns, stationed with the radar operators on the football pitch, were nearer to the radar unit than before. All the fighting Allied troops were on the island now, all of them gathered into a reduced area and more compressed.

That gave the Japanese aircraft a smaller, more populous bombing target than before – and so a far more vulnerable one.

The Japanese bombers encountered no real opposition:

'Our equipment was fitted with a device for identifying Allied aircraft, so as to avoid accidents of friendly fire. But it was never activated – there was never an Allied plane in the sky.'

Meanwhile the enemy convoys of 27, 54 and 108 aircraft flew over repeatedly – almost always flying just above the firing range of the two heavy guns, to devastating effect.

The raids intensified as the intervals between them became shorter. They were practically continuous.

– 8 –
Greatcoats

DESTROYING PART OF THE CAUSEWAY delayed the inevitable, but only for a week. Ten days into February, thousands of Japanese had reached Singapore from the sea.

All radar operators were ordered to leave the island: the security risks of their remaining in the path of the invading enemy – where they could be captured and interrogated about the radar equipment – were too great.

The radar team were to sail from Keppel Harbour.

The football pitch on which they were stationed was close to the harbour, and so they did not have far to go; but when they reached the dockside, there was a problem:

'When we'd first got to Singapore, we'd all arrived with heavy army greatcoats.

Since then – in the tropical heat and now with bombs going off everywhere – we hadn't given our greatcoats a lot of thought. But the strict army mindset was very clear: "You came with greatcoats, so you'll leave with greatcoats."

Those greatcoats were universal issue. They were fine for England or Europe in winter, but not the Far East. As soon as we'd arrived at Changi, the first thing we'd got rid of were our greatcoats, which went into storage at the barracks. We hadn't seen them or thought about them since.

That had been over ten weeks earlier, and a very long ten weeks too. War had broken out, we'd lost Malaya, Singapore was under siege, and now we'd been ordered to leave the island.

But rules were rules. The officials at the harbour were adamant that we couldn't sail without our greatcoats.

So we had to go back to Changi, which is nowhere near Keppel Harbour – it's on a different corner of the island. It was a twenty-six mile truck ride, as I recall.

When we got there the barracks were practically deserted, as you can imagine with everything else that was going on. The staffing there was paper thin and nobody had a clue where our greatcoats were. We spent ages trying to find them. In the end we gave up and thought we'd better return to the Anson Road stadium.

When we got back we tried again at the harbour and explained that we just couldn't find our greatcoats. There were different people on duty by this time and they agreed to let us through.

But we were too late. We hurried onto the dock, just to see the ship pull out of the harbour and sail away.'

What surprised me most was that he seemed more amused than annoyed by his recollection of this incident. The stupidity of insisting on greatcoats at such a time and the havoc that it had caused was, in a way, comical – but the consequences that it had led to were not.

I already had some idea of the ordeals he had had to face later on. If he could have left Singapore in good time, he might have avoided them. Was he not angry?

'They were idiots. But I can't feel too angry now.'

I wondered why not.

'Most of those ships were sunk.'

9

Friday the Thirteenth

BLACK FRIDAY – 13 February 1942 – was Singapore's worst day yet.

The Japanese had repaired the Causeway and sent in their tanks; they had captured the reservoirs and pumping stations which supplied Singapore with its water; and now they had cornered all the Allied forces into a small district in the southernmost part of the island.

The bombs were no longer aimed at main roads and vital supplies, but at the Allies themselves.

With the men packed into one densely populated area, they were in greater danger than ever before:

'The planes came around in enormous numbers from first thing in the morning to last thing at night – just blanket bombing, round and round again over us.

There was a raid while I was walking across the football ground to get to the radar cabin. I could tell that this was going to be an attack aimed specifically at our group – and it was. One of many that day.

I threw myself flat on the ground, to reduce the chances of being blasted away. Then, as the bombs hit the football pitch, I felt a heavy thud on my back – I don't think I was wearing a shirt at the time – and immediately I could feel that I was soaking wet.

I had no doubt at all that I'd been wounded.

Very gingerly, I put my hand onto my back, expecting it to be covered in blood. But it wasn't. I'd just been splattered with wet turf that had been pulled out from the ground where the bombs had fallen. I was okay.'

But the raids went on:

'After I'd got back to the radar cabin, there was another explosion just outside. This one was ear-splitting. The cabin shook with it.

We scampered out to see what had happened. It was terrible: a direct hit on one of our two guns. That was what they'd been trying to do all day and now they'd finally got us.

Just a few moments earlier it had been a massive, rock solid, heavy gun. Now it was smashed to bits.

There'd been nine men operating that gun. We went into the gun pit and saw the mess in there.

All nine of them dead.'

I swallowed hard. I had never heard this before.

'We went back after dark and carried the men's bodies to the Seamen's Mission, which backed onto the football pitch. We dug a single grave for the nine of them in a corner of the front lawn.

We may have put a blanket over each one ... it's hard to remember now. But that's where we laid them to rest.'

He stopped for a few moments. I thought he had finished speaking. But then he added:

'One of the nine was Second Lieutenant Youle.'

10

Surrender

THE MEN WHO HAD GONE INTO THE GUN PIT were badly shaken.

Their commanding officer issued an order for them to take a rest from their duties the following day, and so they spent much of Saturday 14 February in the Seamen's Mission – too stunned by the awful events of Black Friday to absorb the scale of the bloodbath still going on outside.

Japanese troops stormed Singapore's Alexandra Military Hospital and bayoneted over two hundred patients and staff, in a horrifying orgy of unbridled barbarism. Some of the victims were on operating tables undergoing surgery at the time.

It was a terrifying warning to the Allied high command of the ruthless savagery waiting to be unleashed, should the island continue to hold out.[4]

♦

The gunners and radar operators returned to duty on Sunday 15 February.

The outlook was even grimmer than it had been at the start of Black Friday. The Japanese had made further advances, putting the whole area within range of their artillery. Meanwhile Singapore had undergone a further forty-eight hours of carnage:

---

[4]   It was subsequently claimed that the Japanese troops had been fired at by retreating Indian soldiers taking refuge in the hospital grounds and that the Japanese had gone into the hospital to search for them.

'A few days earlier we'd had a visit to the island from General Wavell, exhorting us to fight to the bitter end.

It was looking as if we were going to do just that. The town was being bombed to smithereens, the streets were full of dead and the bodies were piling up. We couldn't even bury them, because of the constant attacks from the air. There was a mounting risk of disease with no water or sanitation and now they'd captured our food supply.'

It was another day of heavy bombing, until a brief lull at around four in the afternoon. Then more aircraft flew over:

'We couldn't understand why they were flying so low. The Japanese knew the range of our guns and always tried to fly comfortably above it. But these planes were flying about halfway down from that. They were easily within range.

Our remaining gun opened fire but didn't manage to shoot them down – probably because of the surprise of suddenly having something so unexpectedly low to aim at. But it was enough to make the planes break up. They dispersed and flew off in all different directions.'

Soon afterwards an officer came into the radar cabin, to tell the men that an order had been issued by General Percival, the commander of the Allied forces in the region: all secret and technical equipment and documents were to be destroyed immediately.

There could be only one explanation for an order of that sort. General Percival was on his way to Singapore's Ford building to meet with General Yamashita, his Japanese counterpart.

♦

Yamashita thumped the table and demanded an immediate surrender.

He announced that a further onslaught was scheduled for later that evening. The Japanese staff officer had a map open in front of him, which seemed to indicate an attack cutting straight through the southern area where the remaining Allied troops were based and surging all the way through to the sea. An assault of that kind would not only be calamitous for the Allies: it would mean hundreds of thousands of further deaths among the civilian population.

History is still undecided as to whether Yamashita was bluffing, but the events of the previous weeks indicated nothing to suggest that he was. Either way, the Allies' position had become impossible.

Percival signed the surrender terms at 6.10 p.m.

It later emerged that rumours of a surrender had been circulating throughout the day.

Some, on both sides, had mistakenly believed that a ceasefire was due to take effect from as early as 4 p.m. The Japanese aircraft which had flown so low overhead at that time were not bombers at all: just a premature victory flight.

The surrender took effect at 8.30 p.m. that evening. By that time, the unit had demolished their radar set and the operators had burned all their radar notebooks.

♦

The men received their orders to return to Changi Barracks.

Ben and thousands of others set out through the heat with their heavy haversacks on the twenty-six mile march back to where they had started.

As they wearily made their way through the town, they saw that many of the local population had already used whatever sheets and cloths they could lay their hands on to make Japanese flags:

'They hung them from their windows, and scowled and jeered at us as we went past.

Our day was over. The Japanese were the masters now.'

It was Ben's third time at Changi.

During his first stay, they had been 'very fine barracks' with 'all mod cons'. On his second visit (when he had returned to look for his greatcoat), they had been practically deserted. Now, only a few days later, they were overcrowded to breaking point.

Tens of thousands of defeated Allied troops had converged there at the orders of the Japanese. The place was heaving.

It was chaos. Previously each bed had had its own mosquito net, with a clear gap of two yards separating one bed from the next to avoid infection. Now everybody slept on the floors, with no space between one man and the next.

Those who could not fit into the buildings slept on the balconies – the same balconies from which they had viewed that first air raid on Singapore in early December. The balconies were just as crowded as the insides of the barracks, so others slept on the ground outside.

All these men were now prisoners of the Japanese. There were further prisoners in nearby Changi Jail, where civilians were being held, and there were prisoners in Malaya too. Some 130,000 Allied military personnel were now captives in Japanese hands.

Churchill's verdict was blunt: the 'worst disaster' and 'largest capitulation' in British history.

The second part of that, at least, was true.

◆

A few days later, the men were ordered to go into central Singapore:

'We had to line both sides of the main road while Yamashita and his high officers drove down in open vehicles. A victory parade. It was his big day and he was making the most of it.

The whole thing was for his glory and our humiliation. We hated every moment.'

Ben spent the next few weeks at Changi Barracks, but he soon learned what was going on outside:

'The Japanese demanded that we carry out certain tasks for them, and so our officers would select groups of prisoners from Changi – 'work parties' – to go out and do those jobs.

One of the first of these was to clean up all the mess and the chaos that the Japanese had created on the streets. I wasn't selected for that, but the men who were chosen had to go out and clear away all the rubble, the dead bodies and so on.

In the evening, they came back to the barracks and told us what they'd seen: the Japanese had beheaded hundreds of local Chinese and impaled their heads on spikes. Their severed heads were on display in prominent parts of the city, to intimidate the local population.

The message was obvious: "You do what we tell you, or you'll finish up like that."'

The purge continued. Thousands of Chinese were being rounded up and beheaded, bayoneted, or carted away.

Prisoners saw them being marched, blindfolded, towards the beach at Changi; later, the barracks echoed with the sound of machine-gun fire. They were being lined up and slaughtered on other beaches too.

◆

Six weeks after the fall of Singapore, the Japanese issued their first demand for a work party of Allied prisoners to go overseas:

'They wanted a thousand of us to go. I don't know why our regiment was selected for it. There was a rumour that the colonels drew lots and that Hugonin got the short straw.'

On 4 April 1942, Ben became one of a thousand men who boarded the *Nisshu Maru* for an unknown destination.

He would never return to Singapore.

Part Three

Paris of the Orient

'We were told we should be grateful to the
Imperial Japanese Army for sparing our miserable
lives. We were beneath consideration for having
surrendered – but we were lucky: we could redeem our
souls and work hard for the Emperor.'

British prisoner of the Japanese
sent to work on the Saigon docks

– 11 –
Saigon

A THOUSAND prisoners squeezed onto the *Nisshu Maru*, a dilapidated old coal carrier.

Colonel Hugonin, whose regiment made up most of the thousand men, took charge. Their number included two army doctors with medical orderlies.

The ship had been built to carry cargo – not humans – and was far too small. With so little space on deck, most of the prisoners were forced to spend the vast majority of their days and nights down in the ship's hold.

The hold was caked in coal dust. Instead of beds or hammocks, it had been fitted with three rows of wooden shelves – one low, one medium and one high – running along the full length of each of its longest walls. This meant six long shelves in total: three along the main wall on each side.

At night, the prisoners lay on the packed shelves with their heads at the wall end, using their kit bags as improvised pillows; their feet pointed inwards towards the narrow central gangway. Sleep was barely attainable in the stifling humidity and suffocating lack of space, and the days were no better:

'When you sat on the edge of your shelf, you had to hunch down so that your head didn't hit the ceiling or the shelf above you. You'd also find yourself looking smack into the face of the person on the shelf opposite – it was a very narrow gangway.

When we lay down, our arms touched those of the people either side of us, while the taller men found that their feet touched those of the men on the opposite shelf.'

The prisoners had one meal a day: a ball of rice – small enough for a man to be able to cup it inside his hands – with some vegetable shreds, a little meat and some green tea.

The ship had one available water spout, operated by a simple handle. There was a permanent queue for it, with most prisoners managing briefly to rinse their hands and faces once a day.

The toilets were worse: outdoor wooden boxes hanging over the sides of the ship at deck level. The underside of each of the boxes had an opening, and several times a day they were hosed down with sea water; depending on the wind direction, the soiled water and accumulated filth of the used boxes could splatter anywhere – and onto anyone.

At night, a metal drum was placed in the hold to serve the same purpose. The difficulty was trying to find it in the pitch dark – or being able to move at all for the overcrowding.

'We really weren't used to any of this, but that was how we lived for the next six days.

By the time we reached our destination, nearly half of us on the ship – including me – had dysentery.'

The destination, it turned out, was Saigon: 'Paris of the Orient'.

◆

Saigon (or Ho Chi Minh City as it is called today) was the largest city in Vietnam.

Less than two years earlier, the entire region – Vietnam, Cambodia and Laos – had been French territory.[5] On paper, it still was: the area still bore the name French Indo-China. But, for the past eighteen months, the colony's French authorities had been little more than figureheads. The Japanese had moved in from China and were doing largely as they pleased.

---

5   Map on page 20.

It had been a near bloodless invasion. Hitler's victory over France three months earlier had left the colony cut off from outside help and supplies, and the local French had been powerless to deny the Japanese whatever it was that they wanted in Indo-China.

There had been no full-blown Japanese onslaught like the one on Singapore. None had been necessary.

◆

The *Nisshu Maru* pulled into the Saigon docks.

The prisoners disembarked and were marched a short distance down a road into what looked like stables:

'This was to be our first real POW camp.

We were never very clear about what it had been used for before our arrival – probably a very primitive level of accommodation for desperately poor immigrants to the area, or for locals who were just destitute. It was unbelievably basic.'

There were four large wooden huts. In each of these, along both of the longest walls were two hardboard shelves for sleeping on – one above the other – so that there were four long sleeping shelves in each hut.

Each hut had a central pathway running down the length of it (between the two rows of shelves on either side); it started at an open doorway at one end of the hut and ended at another open doorway at the other. The shelves were six feet deep, and so prisoners would sleep with their heads near the wall and their feet towards the hut's central pathway (as they had on the ship); the pathway itself was three feet wide. The shelves were less cramped than on the ship, but the prisoners' arms still touched.

The camp was derelict and badly overcrowded. The primitive toilets were housed in ramshackle, purpose-built huts (an improvement in that respect on the *Nisshu Maru*), but there were far too few of them – especially with almost half the camp suffering from dysentery.

The officers slept in smaller huts than the other prisoners; there were other buildings too, including the Japanese guardhouse, the cookhouse, the guards' quarters and stores. They were positioned around a central open square, and the entire camp was surrounded by a four-strand barbed wire fence.

Some of the huts were offices. The Japanese office huts formed the camp's nerve centre, while another office was allocated to the British[6] as a base from which to oversee the day-to-day organisation of the men.

There was a separate group of more secluded huts which the doctors designated for the sick:

'Those of us who'd arrived with dysentery reported to the medical orderlies. They took the worst cases into the sick huts, but there wasn't enough room in there for us all. The rest of us – which included me – just stayed in our huts and stuck to cabbage water until things cleared up.'

♦

Each prisoner quickly acquired his own spot in a particular hut and on a particular shelf, so that most men ended up sleeping in the same place night after night.

Ben slept on a lower shelf in Hut 'A' – one of the four main huts. His friend Jack Bunston established himself on the shelf immediately above him; it was a pattern that had begun on the *Dominion Monarch* six months earlier, when Bunston had slept on the bunk above Ben.

'We both had dysentery and spent our first ten to twelve days on those shelves and on the dilapidated camp toilets.
After that I was considered well enough for the docks.'

That was why they had been sent here: to work on the docks.

---

6   The prisoners at Saigon were almost exclusively British. It was not until later that Ben was held with Australians and others.

Some prisoners – like the two doctors and their medical orderlies – remained permanently at the camp to carry out specific roles there. There were also men who worked in the camp's cookhouse, preparing meals from whatever food (mostly rice) was provided. Others dealt with hygiene, keeping the toilets and the rest of the camp as clean as they could.

But Ben was among the vast majority who spent most of their waking hours lifting and carrying cargo on the docks.

◆

The docks had eighteen large warehouses. The Japanese had taken over warehouses 1 to 9 for themselves and left the other nine – numbers 10 to 18 – for the French:

'We were very relieved at first to see that there were French people on the docks. We hoped they might be able to look after us in some way. So, when it seemed safe to do so, we disappeared from our work parties on the Japanese side of the docks and trickled over to the French side.

What we hadn't realised was that these were Vichy French.'

Back in Europe, the French Vichy regime was governing the rump of France left unoccupied by Germany and Italy. They were a puppet government of the Nazis and collaborated with the Germans, implementing the same kinds of racist and oppressive policies as those that Hitler had introduced in his own country.

Given the pact between Germany and Japan, Saigon's Vichy French collaborated with the Japanese in much the same way:

'They wanted to keep in with the Japanese, to make life easy for themselves. They were also vehemently anti-British and certainly didn't care about us or our problems. Those of us who got over to the French part of the docks were given very short shrift; they made it abundantly clear that we were not to go there and that they wanted absolutely nothing to do with us.

We were just lucky they didn't inform our guards that we'd crossed over the line – they'd have done that without a second thought. They showed themselves to be a nasty bunch and we kept well away from them after that.'

Not all the local French were so unsympathetic; there were some who would walk past the camp on a Sunday afternoon and drop boxes of cigarettes just outside – close enough for prisoners to be able to fetch them without being noticed. But it was soon obvious that any locals who became too involved with the prisoners would be taking an enormous risk.

The men increasingly understood how isolated they were. Many missed home more desperately now than at any other time since they had left; Ben, starting on the docks and still weak from his spell of dysentery, was one of them.

◆

Ben was not only missing his family: he was officially *missing*.

Since the fall of Singapore, no information had been received in Britain about what was happening to him or whether he was still alive. The same applied to all the other prisoners; not having ratified the Geneva Convention, the Japanese provided no details.

There was no news either of Second Lieutenant Youle. The direct bomb hit which had killed him and eight others had happened only two chaotic days before the surrender: the Japanese had taken control of Singapore before the awful news of the nine men could be relayed back to Britain.

So Mrs Youle had just as little information regarding her son as Ben's mother had about hers. But, while Ben's mother remained determined not to lose hope, Mrs Youle was convinced beyond question that her own son was dead.

She told Ben's mother why – but I shall return to that later.

12

The New Routine

EACH MORNING AT SIX O'CLOCK, the men were woken by the sound of the Japanese bugle call. The day followed a set pattern from then on.

A small group of designated prisoners collected the rations from the cookhouse and put them onto four outdoor tables – one outside each of the four large huts. The rest of the prisoners queued up at the tables with their mess tins and water bottles.

It was predominantly rice – about a handful per prisoner – usually accompanied by an even smaller quantity of sugar or maize, and half a pint of tea or boiled water. When they had received their helpings, the men took them back to their huts where they sat and ate from their mess tins. It did not take long.

Then there was another bugle call, this time for *'Tenko'*. To all intents and purposes, *'Tenko'* meant 'roll call', except that there was no calling out of names from a register. It was just a headcount by the Japanese guards.

When the bugle sounded for *Tenko*, the men had to assemble on the open camp square in a number of set formations so that they could be counted. One of these formations might, for instance, be a block of four rows of twenty-five prisoners – making a hundred men in that particular group. The process of working out the total number of prisoners on the camp square using this method could go on for some time.

There would never be the full thousand, because of the prisoners who were too ill to attend *Tenko*. Some of the Japanese guards would go into the sick huts to count those separately.

'Counting our sick men was the sum total of the interest that the Japanese showed in them. They took a very perfunctory view of the sick – they didn't want to know too much and provided no medicines worth talking about. They'd take rather more of an interest later on, but not in a good way.'

The Japanese officer in charge normally came out onto the camp square at the end of the headcount. He stood on a podium in front of the assembled prisoners and usually had an announcement to make. When he had finished, all the prisoners had to salute him and *Tenko* would be dismissed.

The prisoners then split up into their different work parties to be marched off to the nearby docks.

The work mostly involved loading and unloading heavy crates and sacks, and carrying them between the ships and the warehouses (or directly from the incoming ships onto railway trucks, to be transported to some other destination).

When the warehouses became full, the prisoners would have to start stacking the crates on the dockside:

'The trick was to start off with a large base, so that there were as many crates on the lowest level of the stack as possible. Then the next level up would have very slightly fewer crates, the next level after that very slightly fewer again, and so on.'

This way, the crates on the outside edges of the stack formed steps which the prisoners could climb up, so that they could pile up more crates as the stack grew higher and higher.

At around noon, when the sun was high in the sky, a small advance party of prisoners would return to the camp cookhouse and carry the midday food to the four serving tables outside the huts – as they had at breakfast. Again it was a modest portion of rice for each man, this time with some vegetable stew and another half pint of tea or boiled water.

Meanwhile the other prisoners, still on the docks, would be preparing to return to the camp for their lunch. If they had built an outdoor crate stack, they would have to pull a tarpaulin over it to protect the contents from any sudden monsoon:

'On one occasion I was on the stack, probably about fifteen to twenty feet above the ground, pulling the tarpaulin over the crates. I took a step back to pull it tight but there was no crate underneath me where there should have been and I ended up doing a double somersault down to the ground.

It was agony. I had to be helped up off the ground and back to the camp, arm over shoulder, with someone on each side.

Luckily I'd fallen flat on my back, so the pain didn't last too long and nothing was broken. But we had a lot of injured men in the sick huts because of accidents like that.'

After their midday meal at the camp, the men were lined up again and marched back in their work parties to the docks for their afternoon's work.

As well as the crates and boxes, there were fifty-gallon drums of petrol which the prisoners would turn on their sides and roll along the ground – initially by kicking them, but later they found it easier to manoeuvre them by prodding them along with sticks.

Then there were the huge sacks of rice, salt and sugar. A single sack was meant to weigh a hundred kilograms; this was roughly sixteen stone, but in reality it was heavier because of the moisture absorbed from the surrounding humidity.

They were long sacks, and several prisoners would carry one together – each lowering his head slightly to support its weight on the back of his neck and upper back. If any one of the prisoners momentarily fell out of step with the others, the whole group could be thrown off balance.

♦

At some time after six in the evening, the men would be lined up on the docks and marched back to the camp.

The third and final meal of the day involved the same procedure for the prisoners as the other two: queuing at the tables with their mess tins and water bottles and then taking the food back to the huts to eat on their shelves.

'It was much like the previous two meals – predominantly rice, with half a pint of tea.

Also perhaps some thin meat stew, but it would be very watery because the cookhouse had so little meat. They diced it into small cubes; we'd be lucky to get a helping with more than one or two cubes of meat in it – about the size of sugar lumps.'

Afterwards the bugle would sound for evening *Tenko*, so that the guards could satisfy themselves that everyone who was supposed to have returned to the camp had come back. Once *Tenko* was over, the men had what was left of the day to themselves.

Prisoners who had been on the docks would queue to rinse themselves down under the murky water from the outdoor taps. There was not much else to do on the camp afterwards.

The evening wore on, with very little happening – at least in the early days – until the tired and hungry prisoners finally returned to their crowded shelves for the night.

Tomorrow would be the same again.

♦

This pattern repeated itself for ten consecutive days, at the end of which a prisoner was entitled to one rest day on the camp.

After that he would return to the docks for another ten days' work.

13

No Escape

EIGHT WEEKS after reaching Saigon, two of the camp's younger prisoners decided to escape.

Tucker and Wade made a hole in the camp's wire fence and climbed out at night. They had a plan, but it quickly unravelled and they were betrayed to the Japanese military police.

Tucker and Wade were brought back to the camp, tied up and interrogated. Afterwards they were made to kneel on the hard floor all night under close watch, without food or water.

The next day they were exhibited outside the guardhouse, standing in the blazing sun with their hands tied behind their backs. Ben saw them there, as did practically everyone else on the camp: the guardhouse was very prominent and the prisoners had to go past it every time they went to or from the docks.

Tucker and Wade were then removed from the camp to be incarcerated in Saigon's Cholon Jail.

Six weeks later, a party of men were allowed to attend the burial of a prisoner – by no means the first – who had died of dysentery. They went to the local civilian cemetery.

There they saw an unmarked plot, with two mounds. It was a shallow grave: so shallow that it stank of rotting flesh.

That afternoon, the Japanese commandant summoned Colonel Hugonin and confirmed to him what everyone now suspected. Three days earlier, Tucker and Wade – badly beaten and tortured at Cholon Jail – had been marched into the local cemetery and made to dig their own grave. They were either shot or beheaded.

After that, any prisoner intending to sneak out of the camp – even briefly – needed nerves of steel. Basil Bancroft had them.

He regularly climbed through the wire fence at night and went into Saigon. There he made friends among the more sympathetic of the local French population; he was understood also to have one or more girlfriends there. The trips became increasingly frequent, but he was always back before morning.

Basil Bancroft was less at risk of being spotted than Tucker and Wade had been, because he always returned before daylight. But Bancroft, who was South African born, also had something else in his favour: he was black. As one of only three black men out of the thousand, he did not have the appearance that most locals associated with being an Allied prisoner of war.

On his return, he usually brought some food or medical supplies back to the camp with him. Practically all the prisoners knew about his night-time excursions. None of the guards did.

Many months later, the pattern changed. Morning arrived and Basil Bancroft had not returned.

The prisoners managed to cover up for him at morning *Tenko* by engineering some kind of a confusion with the numbers in the sick huts, which muddled the headcount. They pulled off the same trick at evening *Tenko* too.

Bancroft did not return the next day either. It became increasingly difficult to keep repeating the same manoeuvre with the sick hut numbers, and so new ways of distorting the headcount had to be found.

The longer it went on, the harder it became to continue concealing that they were one man down. Bancroft had stood out more than any other prisoner on the camp, because of his dark skin and exceptionally heavy build: it was only a matter of time before the guards would realise that they had not seen him for a while. The risks of trying to manipulate the headcount indefinitely – with catastrophic consequences if they were caught – were becoming increasingly difficult to justify, and so the Japanese commandant was informed that a prisoner had left.

Early the next morning, Basil Bancroft reappeared on the camp. It turned out that he had overslept on the first night of his absence and had then decided to extend his break. Now he was back.

A secret meeting was convened in the sick huts – the part of the camp in which the guards took the least interest – where Bancroft was told what had happened while he had been gone. He was confronted with a stark choice: he could stay on the camp and meet the same awful fate as Tucker and Wade, or he could leave before the guards saw him and try his luck outside.

Bancroft went through the wire one last time, never to return.

◆

'I told Larry that I wasn't going to be leaving my car in his parking lot any more. He wasn't looking after it or any of the other cars there so far as I could see. It was on an old bomb site and kids loitered around there scraping the cars' bonnets and causing other kinds of damage. It wasn't even all that convenient for the office.'

This was an incident that had happened in London several years after the war. It did not interest me in the least.

'So I went back to parking it on the streets – it wasn't so difficult to find a space in those days.

On one occasion I parked in the Bloomsbury area and as I was getting out of the car, across the other side of the street, there was Basil Bancroft! We saw each other and recognised each other immediately. My heart missed a few beats – I was astonished to see him.

We stopped and had a long chat. He was working as a janitor, I think, at one of the university buildings. We swapped addresses and I told him about our annual Saigon reunions that we'd started to hold. He said he'd love to come along, and for very many years he did.

He died not long ago.'

Basil Bancroft's friends in Saigon had taken him to the north of French Indo-China and handed him across the Chinese border to sympathetic locals. Anti-Japanese sentiment in China had enabled him to move in stages all the way up to the north, where he had crossed the border into Russia. He had been free to travel west across Russia – Britain's ally against Hitler – and from there he had sailed to England.

Bancroft's physical appearance and his contacts in the area had placed him in a unique position.

Practically any other prisoner trying to escape was bound to be recaptured and – even if he was not – others might be put at risk. There could be repercussions for his friends, workmates, the men who slept adjacent to him and his hut orderlies – perhaps the whole camp.

Escape was out of the question.

♦

The daily grind on the docks continued and intensified as the volume of work increased.

The Japanese had dominance over the whole of the Pacific Ocean and would have as many as thirty ships come in at a time. The prisoners had been on the docks for ten hours a day from the start, but now there was still more work to be done.

So the Japanese began requiring parties of prisoners to work at night. This was in addition to their daytime hours:

'That meant going back onto the docks after evening Tenko *and not returning to the camp until very late – often two or three in the morning.*

We'd have some rice and water when we got back and then climb onto our shelves, worn out, for what was left of the night.

We had to get up again at six.'

It happened frequently. During busy periods, Ben found himself working two or three nights a week.

14

Prison Life

THE PRISON HIERARCHY placed the lowest-ranking guard above the highest-ranking prisoner of war. Camp life was designed so as constantly to remind every prisoner of that fact.

Even Colonel Hugonin was made to salute every Japanese guard of every rank – not just in specific circumstances or on certain set occasions, but whenever a guard came into sight.

It was not only the Japanese guards to whom this applied. Many of the guards were Korean:

'The Koreans came a long way below the Japanese in the pecking order, but we all had to salute them too. We'd find out soon enough if we forgot to salute one of them or if we just hadn't seen one coming.'

The Japanese had been in occupation of Korea for over thirty years, and they treated the Koreans as a subject people. More recently Koreans had been recruited into the Japanese military, but the Japanese tended not to trust them as soldiers and so a great many had ended up instead as prison camp guards.

'They'd suffered appallingly at the hands of the Japanese, and we might naturally have been inclined to have some sympathy for them. But they made that very difficult: they certainly had no sympathy for us.

Most of the Korean guards treated us even more viciously than the Japanese guards did. They'd been kicked about for years and now they had us to kick.'

The form of salute required was a stiff downward bow from the waist. A complex and nuanced convention of bowing – with equals bowing to each other – was an accepted social courtesy in Japanese and Korean circles, but for Western prisoners to be forced to bow to every guard in this way was a clear and deliberate humiliation.

Worse than that, however, were the gratuitously ferocious kickings and beatings routinely meted out as punishment for not bowing to a guard when he came into view. Usually in these circumstances the prisoner had simply not seen the guard, or the prisoner had bowed but the guard had not seen him bow (or claimed not to have done).

◆

After ten consecutive days on the docks, a prisoner was paid the local currency equivalent of ten old pence, from which the British administration office deducted three pence at source to purchase supplies for the sick huts.

The remaining seven pence amounted to no more than token 'pocket money' for spending in the camp shop. This was less than any known concept of a minimum wage – even before taking into account the additional unpaid night shifts – but the guards were low-paid too.

However, there was another important factor here which applied only to the prisoners: they were unable to spend their money anywhere except for in the camp shop, which charged inflated prices. The cost of buying anything from the camp shop was considerably more than the Japanese had paid to acquire it locally, and so the Japanese were effectively using the shop to make a profit from the prisoners and to claw their pay back from them.

The result was that a prisoner could spend all of his pay on extra food from the camp shop (which meant doing without other essentials such as soap or toothpowder) and yet still be constantly hungry.

A temporary solution to this problem surfaced when some of the local Vietnamese started to appear in the prisoners' huts. They had found a way into the camp without being detected, and wanted to buy Western goods from the men.

Most of the prisoners – including Ben – were so desperate to buy more food from the shop that they sold them their spare shirts and shorts. Some sold them other possessions which they had been keeping in their kit bags, such as watches or pens.

As a result, the prisoners started to spend more money in the camp shop than they had been paid for their work. When the Japanese saw the increase in the shop's takings, they asked the British adjutant where the men's extra money was coming from:

'He couldn't tell them about our Vietnamese visitors, because that would lead to increased security and probably repercussions for the local people.

And he certainly couldn't say that we'd been selling things to them. Any kind of dealings with the locals was prohibited.

So instead he replied that we'd been selling some of our belongings to the Japanese guards – which was allowed.'

This was a believable explanation, but it gave the Japanese commandant cause for concern. Relatively mundane items, such as Parker pens, were coveted possessions in the Far East and could fetch substantial sums. The prisoners might use these to bribe some of the guards, or to buy the support of local Asians and enlist their help against the Japanese – whether in trying to escape or in any other way.

So the commandant issued an order that all prisoners must hand in their valuables to the guardhouse:

'I had a gold signet ring that my father had given to me when I'd left school ten years earlier. I knew that if I handed it in I'd never see it again and was determined to hold onto it.

The answer to the problem, I decided, lay in my army shaving brush.'

The shaving brush was of no monetary value and – with no razors on the camp – was of no use as a shaving brush either.[7]

'It was just an old shaving brush – they wouldn't expect me to hand it in. So I sat down on the shelf where I slept and used a screwdriver – I think I must have borrowed it from one of the other POWs – to take the shaving brush apart.'

The shaving brush had a large wooden handle. At one end of the handle was a zinc cover into which the bristles had been fixed and secured from the inside.

He slowly prised the zinc cover away from the handle until it came off, leaving exposed the end of the wood that was normally covered by the zinc. He used the screwdriver to pick at that end of the handle and gradually dig a cavity into it that was large enough to hold his ring.

'Then I put the ring inside it. The hole that I'd made wasn't much bigger than the ring, but there was still enough room in there for the ring to move. If the guards carried out a search of our huts, they might notice that the shaving brush rattled.'

So he filled the rest of the cavity with earth from the ground, packing as much of it into the space as he could until the ring could not possibly move inside.

After that he put the zinc cover back onto the handle and very carefully tapped it back on all around the edge, so that the zinc gripped the handle as it had done before he had removed it.

♦

---

[7]   In the absence of razors one of the prisoners, who had been a barber in civilian life, gave each of the men a weekly shave using a shortened kitchen knife which he sharpened with a strip of leather. Ben, being on good terms with him, managed to have a shave every other day.

As the docks became busier, the prisoners had more crates and heavy boxes to carry. It took two men to carry the larger crates, each supporting the crate on one of his shoulders; for a smaller crate, a prisoner would walk with his head jutting forwards so that the crate rested on his upper back.

To prevent the crates from tearing into their skin, the men took off their shirts and folded them into pads to rest the crates on. The pressure and rubbing of the crates soon wore out the shirt material, and as they had no other shirts (having sold them to the local Vietnamese) they started to use their hats as padding instead – until the hats became worn away too.

Their shorts lasted longer, but eventually they needed repair. When a hole appeared in a prisoner's shorts, he would have to find a piece of material from somewhere (often the remnants of a shirt or hat) that he could use to patch over it.

There was a coarse type of thread on the camp and some improvised needles – not purpose-made, but nails rubbed down and adapted by some of the prisoners.

'The new patch often then became the strongest part of the shorts and would pull on the rest of the material, so that further patches had to be sewn on around it. We ended up wearing shorts that were just collections of these patches, with none of the original shorts left.'

♦

Many of the men were still suffering from the dysentery that they had contracted on the *Nisshu Maru,* while further numbers were being admitted to the sick huts as a consequence of the poor diet. Other prisoners had malaria, or could not work due to injuries that they had suffered on the docks.

The rest toiled on under the hot tropical sun with their heads unprotected, their shirts disintegrating, and little to eat or drink.

15

Sparks

ONE MORNING, a French resident of the city called Emile Lienard came onto the Japanese side of the docks. When he felt it was safe to do so, he approached some of the prisoners.

Lienard was from northern France and had an important job with Saigon's electricity and water supply authority. He had gone onto the docks to find the prisoners, as he wanted to help.

'Sparks' (as he later became known to the men) knew everything about Saigon's water and electrical systems; consequently the Japanese depended on him and gave him free rein to roam around the city at will. He knew that he could use this freedom of movement to benefit the prisoners, so long as he was careful: he just needed to be able to pretend that his reason for being in any particular place at any given time was to check some electrical connection or water pipe in the area.

That was how he had managed to wander casually onto the Japanese side of the docks that day, when most other locals would have found it hard to explain why they were there.

He still needed to be cautious, however, so he made contact with only a couple of the prisoners on the docks and did so in a low-key manner, away from the Japanese.

He spoke no English, but the men understood that he was on their side. Soon they were joined by some other prisoners who took an interest in what was going on; only a few moments later, Sparks was being besieged by a crowd of them. Sparks was suddenly at enormous risk.

Luckily the Japanese on the docks did not notice this group of prisoners all flocking around one man; but Colonel Hugonin, who was standing on the dockside and was keeping an eye on everything that went on there, did.

Having seen the incident, Hugonin put out an order that no prisoner should contact or speak to Sparks with the exception of Jack Bunston or, if Jack Bunston was unavailable, then Ben. Bunston was chosen because he spoke reasonable French; Ben's French was based on what he could remember from school: grammatically more correct than Bunston's, but not as useful in practice.

'Sparks proved to be invaluable to us. For one thing, he provided us with news of what was going on in the war.

The Japanese starved us of news and prohibited us from having radio sets. Sometimes the guards would appear in our huts to conduct a search and make sure we didn't have any.'

So the good news was that Sparks provided news; the bad news was that Sparks provided mainly bad news. Matters had not improved in Europe and the Japanese were further tightening their grip in the Far East; since the fall of Singapore, they had taken the Dutch East Indies and the Philippines. They had also seized another British territory: Burma.

'He also collected money for us from his friends and others in Saigon. And he brought in medical supplies – of which the Japanese were providing virtually nothing.'

Sparks arranged a night-time 'drop' of bulk food outside the camp's barbed wire fence near the sick huts. It was brought into the camp over the wire, under the cover of darkness.

Later on, he provided clothing:

'How he organised it I don't know, but he came into the docks and left a huge stack of shorts behind the toilets there. We needed to get them back to the camp without arousing any kind of suspicion, so we each put a pair on over the shorts that we

*were wearing, then another pair over that, and so on. We
marched back to the camp when work was finished wearing five
pairs of shorts each.'*

It was after this incident that Sparks came under suspicion
and was reported to the French authorities.

Fortunately the Commissaire de Police du Port arranged
matters in his favour, and Sparks continued to help the prisoners
for the rest of the war. Sparks was later awarded the King's
Medal for Courage in the Cause of Freedom, by George VI.

♦

One of the first steps that Sparks took was to ask for a nominal
roll of all the camp's prisoners with their names, addresses and
next of kin. A list was secretly passed to him.

Sparks had the list microfilmed so that it was reduced to three
tiny photographic images, which were then handed to a Swiss
diplomat who was leaving Saigon. The diplomat and his wife
travelled home with them sewn into their clothes. Once they
were back in Switzerland, they had the photographs enlarged
back to full size and sent them to the War Office in London.

In late September 1942, a letter from the War Office was
delivered to Ben's mother's address in Edgware.

The family's reaction on receiving it was the same as that of
most of the other thousand households to whom similar letters
had been sent: trepidation, followed by immense relief.

The letter stated that, according to an unofficial list that had
been received, Ben had been alive in May and was a captive in
Japanese hands.

But the uncertainty and the anxiety soon resurfaced. The list
was already four months old and the family still had no idea of
where he was or what was happening to him. Nothing reassuring
was known about how the Japanese treated their prisoners; the
atrocities committed in China gave no cause for optimism.

16

Under Duress

COLONEL HUGONIN regularly went onto the docks – not to fetch and carry, but to observe what was happening and to monitor the treatment of his men.

One afternoon a ship pulled in carrying armaments. They appeared to be British guns captured from Singapore, presumably for use against the Allies. The ship docked and the men were told to unload.

Hugonin intervened. He stood directly between the other prisoners and the ship, and told the Japanese overseer that his men would not handle any of its contents. The overseer bawled back at him but Hugonin remained steadfast. They had clearly reached an impasse; the prisoners were ordered to fall into line and everyone was marched back to the camp.

The men waited on the camp square as the Japanese commandant was brought out from his office hut to see the colonel. Hugonin was joined by his adjutant, Captain Faraday; Major Parr, the British interpreter, was caught awkwardly in the middle of the confrontation, translating for both sides.

Colonel Hugonin was adamant: it was contrary to the Geneva Convention to force prisoners to work for the enemy war effort. The commandant answered that the convention had nothing to do with Japan. (He was right, in the sense that Japan had never ratified it, but that clearly did not solve the problem.) Hugonin, supported by Faraday, stood his ground.

Rather than prolong his exchange with Hugonin and Faraday, the commandant turned to his own guards and gave them an order in Japanese; immediately the guards left the central area of the camp ground, all going off in different directions. An uncomfortable silence followed, as the prisoners stood on the camp square waiting to see what would happen.

Then four huge machine guns appeared. The guards positioned one machine gun in each of the four corners of the square, with all four guns pointing inwards at the prisoners.

The commandant addressed his next words directly to Hugonin. As he spoke, he pointed to the guns and made a dramatic sweeping motion with his arm, as if to indicate the assembled prisoners' imminent demise. There was no need for Major Parr to translate.

Hugonin and Faraday moved several yards away, so that they could confer privately – or as privately as was possible with the entire camp standing there. Faraday, a solicitor from Taunton, was accustomed to dealing with knotty legal conundrums, but not many as knotty as this one; yet he was sensible enough to know when to adopt a pragmatic line and Hugonin, a career soldier, valued his judgment.

After a few minutes the two men gestured to Major Parr, who came over to them. They spoke to Parr, who then walked back to the camp commandant to advise him of their decision. The commandant made a signal to the camp guards. The machine guns were withdrawn and the prisoners marched back to the docks to do as they had been told.

Hugonin and Faraday stayed behind.

When the prisoners returned again at the end of the day, they saw something that had not been there when they had left a few hours earlier: two tiny mud huts on the camp square.

Inside one of the two huts was Colonel Hugonin; he had barely enough room in there to breathe, let alone move. In the other was Captain Faraday.

'They were kept imprisoned in there for a day or so – it was their punishment for standing up to their captors. Bizarrely, the

guards had built those mud cases around the two men, on the spot, as they'd stood there. They'd done it just as we'd been heading back to the docks following the earlier confrontation. It had all happened extremely quickly – by all accounts they'd finished them in just a few minutes.'

◆

After that, Hugonin mysteriously acquired a stick which he would carry with him as he walked up and down the docks:

'I don't know where he got hold of it. Surprisingly, though, the Japanese never seemed at all curious about why he had suddenly taken to using a stick when he appeared to be a perfectly fit man.'

Perhaps they just thought that walking around with a stick was something senior British officers liked to do in front of their men. But that was not the reason:

'Whenever a shipment of guns came into the docks, he'd casually stroll towards it to get as near as possible. Then he'd have a quick look around to check he wasn't in danger of being spotted. If the coast was clear, he'd jab the stick into a sensitive part of the equipment where it would do as much damage as possible – he had a very good knowledge of guns and how they worked. He never got found out.'

◆

There was a further incident some weeks later:

'The Japanese commandant had received his orders from higher up the chain that he was to obtain from every one of us a signed declaration that we wouldn't try to escape.

The whole idea of trying to escape was theoretical, of course. No white prisoner was likely to take that risk after what had happened to Tucker and Wade.

But we were still required under King's Rules and Regulations at least to try to escape if we could. We'd be in breach of army law if we signed a declaration promising to stay put, and could be court-martialled if the declaration was ever produced in evidence.'

Colonel Hugonin and Captain Faraday refused to permit any of their men to sign. When the prisoners returned from the docks that day, they learned that Hugonin and Faraday had been locked up in the camp's 'no-good soldiers house': a tiny hut, measuring only five foot square and six feet high.

Matters deteriorated further when the commandant announced that there would be no food for the prisoners until they had all signed.

'In the end a formula was agreed where we were allowed to sign our names but add 'signed under duress'.

The Japanese understood that those words robbed our declarations of any legal force, but they still accepted it. They knew there was no real chance of any of us escaping anyway.'

♦

There were still nearly sixteen thousand prisoners at Changi. They, too, were refusing to sign a 'no escape' declaration after four men had tried unsuccessfully to escape (leading to the same fate for those four as had been meted out to Tucker and Wade).

Changi's prisoners were forced to stand on a parade ground built to hold only one-twentieth of their number. They were to remain there, with hardly any water and no sanitation, until they caved in.

Three days later, the men were still holding out – though many had collapsed from heat and thirst, and some had died.

That was when the Japanese announced their decision to bring the diphtheria cases out of the hospital to join them. This amounted to a threat of execution and, therefore, duress.

The men signed – many of them using false names.

17

Crime and Punishment

A STACK of tinned food had gone missing.

The regiment had brought the tins with them from Singapore. Shortly after reaching Saigon, Colonel Hugonin had ordered that they be kept in the cookhouse so that, if the prisoners were still there on Christmas Day, they could at least have something more than the usual rice to eat. Now they were gone.

Hugonin conducted an inquiry to find out who had taken the food. It turned out that three prisoners had stolen it; two of them were regular soldiers who were widely known to have been in trouble with the law when they had first joined up. Fortunately the food was still on the camp (some of it in the prisoners' kit bags) and it was returned to the cookhouse.

Colonel Hugonin was determined to prevent an atmosphere of lawlessness from developing among the prisoners, and so the retrieval of the food could not be the end of the matter. He arranged with the guards for the three men to be placed in an area of confinement within the camp, where they remained for several days and were then released.

♦

Stealing from the Japanese was an entirely different matter – so much so that it was not generally referred to as 'stealing' at all.

It was called 'ponging' – or 're-taking from the enemy' – and it happened all day long on the docks:

'Practically all of us ponged whatever we could whenever we could. We were constantly hungry.

Sacks, parcels, boxes – we made it our business to find out what was in them. If the coast was clear, we'd drop a crate in the hope that the seal would break and we could see what was in it.

We'd want it to contain food of course – food that would otherwise have gone to feed Japanese soldiers somewhere else. If we hit lucky and it was the kind of food that we could quickly shove into our pockets – tinned food was ideal – then we would. If there was anything we could usefully pong, we ponged it.'

As well as food, they might find medical supplies – or something else:

'I managed to get into a box which had various bits and pieces in it – comforts for the Japanese troops who were fighting against us in Burma. Many of the contents were too big to go in my pockets, but there was one particular item – a roll of film – that I was especially curious about, and so I took it.'

When he was back at the camp, he held the film up to the light.

It was a movie reel showing a small group of British officers, all in tropical uniform, walking along a road. One of them had a Union Jack over his shoulder; another was carrying a white flag. The tallest and lankiest of the group, slightly ahead of the others, appeared to be General Percival.

'I couldn't believe what I'd found. It was Singapore, a few months earlier. They were on their way to surrender to General Yamashita.

I kept it very well hidden from the guards for the whole of my time in Saigon. One day I was going to bring this home.'

The surrender footage had been filmed at the time by Japanese photographers; now it was being widely distributed to boost the morale of Japanese troops fighting overseas.

'We also ponged at the fish factory – probably in both senses of the word.'

The fish factory was at the far end of the Japanese side of the docks and was smaller than any of the warehouses. Every morning, fishing trawlers came into the docks and a group of prisoners would be ordered to unload the fish from the boats into containers and bring them into the fish factory.

These prisoners then had the job of taking the fish out of the containers, putting them onto a slab, and slicing their heads off with sharp knives. Next they gutted and cleaned the fish bodies, before dropping them into buckets of brine so that they could be put into cold storage. Then the fish would be sent to the Japanese troops in Burma.

'After a while, we had an idea. Instead of just cutting the heads off and throwing them away, we started to cut the fish about half an inch beneath the head. Then we put the heads in our pockets and took them back to the camp, knowing that there was that half an inch of fish on each of them.'

They continued doing this for some time. But then:

'At around noon one day, we were lined up on the docks to be marched back for our midday rice. There were about twenty of us standing together with our pockets full of fish heads. We weren't too worried about it – we'd never been caught yet. But this time the guards unexpectedly decided that they were going to search us.

So we all frantically emptied our pockets – and suddenly there was a spectacular volley of fish heads through the air around us!'

He laughed as he told me this, and I found it funny too. But what interested me more was that his general air of amusement continued into this final phase of the anecdote:

'Well, the guards saw this and they went mad. We all got beaten around the face for it then and there. That was what we called "getting a chilli", because our ears would turn red from being bashed about.'

I told him I was surprised that he could look back on an incident that had ended in this way with such amusement.

His answer was that beatings were very commonplace – so much so that it was the flying fish heads, rather than having his face repeatedly whacked afterwards, that made this episode memorable.

'The bashings that we had were very frequent. At the slightest excuse they'd let fly with their fists, or just knock us down with their rifle butts and give us a good kicking.'

Not only were prisoners treated in this way: guards were routinely beaten by more senior guards as a matter of normal army discipline. This left the Koreans more at the mercy of these beatings than any Japanese guard was; yet a Korean had as much authority as any Japanese guard did to strike a prisoner.

Consequently, the prisoners bore the brunt.

The most prevalent of these on-the-spot punishments was 'hard-slapping': several blows across the head and face, delivered with a rigid open hand and a straight arm swung briskly from the shoulder. Prisoners soon learned that they had no choice but to stand stiffly to attention and 'take it'; if the prisoner flinched, or tried to roll with it or – worst of all – resist, then a full-scale beating would follow.

There was also guilt by association. When four prisoners were caught taking tins of condensed milk, the remaining thirty-four men in their work party were lined up for some particularly vicious hard-slapping, while the four who had been caught were made to stand in the sun with their hands in the air for half an hour. Afterwards, the four were hard-slapped repeatedly, kicked to the ground and beaten with bamboo sticks.

'Stealing wasn't the only crime, of course. Not bowing to the guards was another – even if we just hadn't seen them.

Or not working as fast as they wanted us to – we'd get knocked about for that as well. We'd taken over from a workforce of more than twice our size, so we were very hard pushed and there were language difficulties too. Just a hesitation on our part while we tried to understand their instructions could send them into a rage.'

♦

There was another activity on the docks, just as widespread among the prisoners as 'ponging': sabotage.

'We did whatever damage we could, when we weren't being watched. We'd loosen the stoppers on the petrol drums, so that their contents drained out, or we'd leave the petrol in there but pour sand into it knowing the harm that would do.

Another ploy was dropping ammunition into the sea while it was being unloaded.

And, being an artillery regiment, a lot of our men had a very good understanding of guns. They'd take the opportunity to tamper with them in all sorts of ways whenever they could.'

That too was punishable – but no more so than 'ponging'.

♦

What was most remarkable to many was the absence of any apparent concept of proportionality.

Ten weeks after arriving, two ravenously hungry prisoners had each taken three bags of biscuits from one of the warehouses. The bags were small enough to fit into their trouser pockets and down their socks unnoticed.

Minutes later, they were searched and found out. The entire work party's pay was stopped for ten days, but that was nothing compared with what happened to the two men.

Following a savage beating in the Japanese dock office, they were tied up into kneeling positions so that moving their ankles pulled on their throats. The dock commandant flogged them repeatedly with his sword scabbard, kicked them with his jackboots, and crushed red cigarette ends on their bare chests.

Next they were made to stand to attention for two hours under the scorching hot sun, without hats and with a sack of biscuits hung around each of their necks – to the evident amusement of many of the guards.

Later they were brought to the camp commandant's office to explain themselves. Their explanation – that they had been hungry – earned them another face-slapping and a night in the camp's tiny 'no-good soldiers house'.

The men were told their punishment the next morning: ten days tied up outside the guardhouse with no food.

Death by starvation.

They stood outside the guardhouse all day with their hands tied behind their backs, and slept on the open ground at night.

After prolonged argument and negotiation, an outraged Colonel Hugonin managed to have the sentences reduced to seven days – an improvement, but still too long. Later in the week, however, one of the more humane guards secretly started giving them food at night, and the two men survived the ordeal.

But the camp commandant warned that any future offenders would be executed by sword – either cut in half from the shoulder down or impaled through the stomach.

♦

If this incident had any deterrent effect at all, it was only short lived. 'Ponging' resumed soon afterwards:

'We ponged whatever we could, and we continued doing it for the rest of our time on the docks. We all knew it was dangerous, but we had to take calculated risks.

We were too hungry not to.'

18

All Men Must Be Happy

ALMOST A YEAR had passed since the *Dominion Monarch* had set sail from Liverpool.

Ben kept being reminded of it by other prisoners who had travelled with him; they increasingly remarked on how much had changed in that one year alone.

For Ben, however, there was a further significance. If nearly twelve months had passed since leaving for Singapore, then the Jewish New Year must be approaching.

It was not difficult to work out when the Jewish New Year would be: each month in the Jewish calendar starts with a new moon, and the sky over the camp was clear enough for Ben to be able to tell when the next one would appear.

There was only one other Jewish prisoner at Saigon. He too was from an observant family; both he and Ben were ill-at-ease about working over the new year. They would have felt differently if their work on the docks had been benefiting the Allies, but clearly it was not.

They decided to speak with the padre.

Padre Todd spent most of his waking hours playing bridge.

He always had a cigarette hanging out of his mouth; perplexingly, he seemed to have an endless supply of them – suggesting that he had either brought a job lot of cigarettes with him from Singapore or secured some other source of supply. The mystery was never solved; it would have been easy enough to ask him, but perhaps it was just not the kind of question that people felt comfortable asking a padre.

He put in an appearance at the sick huts each morning. By all accounts these were cursory visits: the rumour was that he would turn up, lob a couple of cigarettes at each of the patients, and then move on as he was keen to get back to his bridge.

Whether or not this was a fair assessment of Padre Todd (and perhaps it was not), he was certainly sympathetic to Ben and the other Jewish prisoner when they went to see him. They explained their circumstances and said they were happy to make up the time by working extra nights. Padre Todd seemed to have had little or no experience of Jewish people, but he took their concerns seriously and managed to arrange for them to be excused from the docks for those two days.[8]

A year later, the possibility of asking for time off for the Jewish New Year – or for almost anything else – would be unthinkable.

These two characteristics of Padre Todd – cigarettes and religion – were both aspects of life which were more prevalent then than now. The health risks of smoking were not yet known, and more people professed a belief in God.

Before long, these two apparently unconnected themes clashed:

'I was lucky: I found I could give up smoking without too much effort. We had hardly any money to spend in the camp shop, and the tobacco that they sold in there was horrible compared to what we were used to at home.

Most smokers found it harder to stop, so they carried on and got used to the new tobacco. But to smoke it they needed something the shop didn't sell: cigarette paper.'

---

8   The Day of Atonement – or *Yom Kippur* – falls a little over a week after the Jewish New Year; the two men did not need to seek time off for that, as it coincided with a rest day for both of them. (Ben had spent the previous Day of Atonement on the *Dominion Monarch*.)

The smokers did however have a readily available substitute. The thin rice paper on which the bibles in their kit bags were printed was ideal for rolling cigarettes.

It seemed an unthinkable use for a bible, but it was only a matter of taking the first step. After a prisoner had ripped one page out and smoked it, the bible was no longer complete and the spell was broken. It became easier after that: the men got through almost all the pages in their bibles while they were at Saigon.

So smoking triumphed over bible-reading – but what of religion?

'They only destroyed their bibles because they needed to smoke – that was all. Faith remained very important to many of us.

There was always a church service on the camp square on Sunday evenings and those services were very well attended. A lot of the prisoners had their faith rekindled as something to hold onto – an anchor to help survive what was happening to them.

I'd often stand on the edge of the service and listen to Padre Todd delivering his thoughts. I listened to the hymns being sung and, although it was a Christian service, there were some that I could join in – at least in my mind if not vocally: hymns such as Psalm 23 (The Lord is My Shepherd), *or* O God, Our Help in Ages Past.

People varied, of course. But in very many cases I'd say the experience strengthened our beliefs.'

What about a year later, when matters had become a great deal worse?

I forgot to ask him that, but I knew the answer anyway. Increasing numbers lost their faith as conditions deteriorated, but others clung on resolutely (as in his case), or even turned to religion as a means of survival in a way that they had never done before.

The best-attended religious service was the one held on Christmas Day morning.

The Japanese commandant had agreed that the men could have a day's break from the docks, and so after the service the prisoners had a special Christmas lunch: the tinned meats that they had brought with them from Singapore.

Colonel Hugonin addressed the men, standing on a mound of earth where they could see him. It was a supportive Christmas message, and as positive as anything could be under the circumstances.

He opened his comments by alluding to the fact that plans were underway to build an additional *'benjo'* (Japanese for 'toilet') on the mound where he was standing. It was a welcome development, given the clear inadequacy of the camp's existing arrangements.

'So I'm standing on the site of a new *benjo*,' he announced – and then added, after a short pause, 'surrounded by a lot more *benjos.*'

The assembled prisoners collapsed into laughter, to the obvious bafflement of the Japanese guards who flanked Hugonin on either side.

♦

The men returned to work the following day. As 1942 became 1943, life at Saigon continued much as before.

Boredom became a growing problem. The long hours on the docks could be soul-destroying, and there was little to do on the camp in the evenings.

Colonel Hugonin was concerned that this could pose a threat to morale, and so it was decided to start holding evening classes to help prisoners keep their minds occupied:

'I was asked to run a course on book-keeping and accounts. I had a book on the subject in my kit bag, which started at a basic level and would work well for this.'

Not all the prisoners saw lectures on book-keeping as a cure for boredom, but some showed an interest and Ben found himself teaching a class of thirty. The lessons were held in the British camp office, as they took place after dark and that was the only hut (other than the Japanese office) which had adequate electric lighting.

Everything went smoothly until the third lesson:

'Suddenly a group of guards burst in and started shouting at us in Japanese. It was targeted mainly at me as the person who was standing up and taking the class, and I was lucky on this occasion not to get a bashing. It was touch and go.'

Their objection was that a gathering of prisoners was taking place without permission.

'We tried to explain that it was just a harmless evening class, but there was obviously a language problem and so they sent for their interpreter and we sent for ours, Major Parr. Colonel Hugonin and Captain Faraday came too.

When Major Parr got there he explained that the whole thing was innocuous, but they really didn't want to know.

One of them snatched the book out of my hands and looked at it. He was holding it upside down. Then he shouted: "This is anti-Japanese – must stop!" The Japanese interpreter didn't step in to help our cause, so that was the last lesson.'

Three of the officers (two trainee accountants and a bank manager) approached Ben afterwards and asked if he would continue the lessons for them at least. Ben carried on teaching those three for the rest of his time in Saigon.

♦

One of Ben's three accountancy students was an accomplished violinist. His violin had been destroyed in the bombing at Singapore, and so another of the officers (the one who had introduced Ben to Second Lieutenant Youle on board the *Dominion Monarch*) built him a replacement:

'It was remarkable: it looked and sounded just like a professionally built violin. The strings were even made of cat gut, which they'd somehow persuaded one of the guards to obtain for them in Saigon.

And it was put to good use.

Some of the more talented POWs formed themselves into a concert party and would stage shows for the rest of us from time to time.

That violin was a fantastic achievement, but there were also a lot of other acts. Sergeant Kelly singing **Jerusalem**, I remember – marvellous voice – and **The Road to Mandalay**.

There was a drag act too, using costumes stitched together from bits of spare cloth. It was surprisingly convincing. Rumour had it that some of the guards were trying to work out how we'd managed to smuggle women onto the camp.'

Later on, the popularity of the shows backfired:

'We were asleep in our huts when one of the most senior Japanese officers got back to the camp. He'd been out on the town and was the worse for wear – really very drunk – and he made a heck of a racket. We were all dog-tired and desperately needed our sleep. We had to be up at six the next morning for the docks.

But he carried on and made more and more of a disturbance. Then he started shouting: "All men must be happy! All men must be happy!"

He wanted us to put on a show for him then and there. It was an order. So all the singers and entertainers had to get up and perform for him in the middle of the night and the rest of us had to sit and watch the show as if it were daytime.

And all because this stupid man had had too much to drink and staggered in insisting that "All men must be happy!"'

But not all men were happy.

Perhaps none of them were, but two of the prisoners in particular – presumably because they could see no hope – stood out especially.

They were Butcher and Willoughby, and their behaviour could not have been more different:

'Butcher couldn't be controlled. He'd had a responsible, technically demanding job in civilian life, but now something in him had snapped. From morning to night he ran around the camp barefoot like a wild animal, wearing nothing but a towel and just shouting and bawling at everyone. Even at the Japanese guardhouse. The guards got used to him and took no notice.

Willoughby was the complete opposite. He went completely mute – just withdrew into himself. All day he sat on the end of his shelf and barely moved from there. The other prisoners appointed a minder for him: a big hefty man called Ted Briggs – tattooed all over. His job was to look after Willoughby, who'd gone to pieces and couldn't look after himself in any way. He hardly spoke a word, if any at all.'

After the war, Butcher made a full recovery and returned to his former way of life. Some suspected that he had been faking, but Ben remained convinced that he had not.

Ben never found out what became of Willoughby.

♦

There was no known formula for avoiding insanity, but there was a mathematical theorem:

'While I was lugging sacks and crates around on the docks, I would try to prove Pythagoras's theorem to myself in my head.

Most well-educated teenagers know what it is and can apply it, or at least they could do in those days. But proving it – even with a pen and paper – is much, much harder.

I'd been able to do it at school, ten years earlier. Now I distracted myself from the endless tedium on the docks by proving it to myself again in my mind's eye – dropping perpendiculars all over the place and drawing parallel lines in my imagination while I worked.

I'd keep on and on at it in my head – just to keep myself sane. When I got to the end I'd go back to the beginning and try proving it using a different method.'

The theorem itself can be stated as follows:

> The area of any square whose sides are the length of the longest side of a right-angled triangle is equal to the sum of the areas of the two squares whose sides are the respective lengths of the triangle's other two sides.

A cure for boredom? A way to avoid insanity?

Strangely, it seemed, yes. If nothing else, it kept him from thinking about the more disturbing conundrums – the questions that held no answer: How long would this continue? Would he ever go home?

19

Seven Hundred Fit Men

THE SUN hung high over the docks as the men prepared to return to the camp for their midday rice.

The assorted work parties lined up on the quayside to be counted before they could be marched back. An initial tally of Ben's group indicated that they were one man short; yet there were no obvious absences, and so the headcount was repeated. They were definitely one down.

Then somebody realised who was missing: Lofty Duggan. Another prisoner said he remembered seeing Lofty dive into the river a few minutes earlier, just after the men had been ordered to line up for their return to the camp. Lofty had wanted to have a quick cool down from his morning's work before going back.

The area where the prisoner had seen Lofty dive in was between two barges. Both the barges were moored against the wall of the dockside; sprawling between them and draped beneath the waterline was an enormous fishing net – a huge stocking immersed in the river and tied to a barge at each end.

A man and a woman were sitting on one of the two barges, resting where they could be shielded from the midday sun. They had fallen asleep and so had not seen what had happened.

'We climbed frantically onto the barge and shook the two of them awake. They were startled for a moment but reacted fast.

The two of them got up and started pulling the net in and then, as the netting came up out of the water, there was Lofty Duggan – caught in the net and trapped.

He'd got in, but he couldn't get out. He was dead.'

Fifteen months after reaching Saigon, there had been almost thirty deaths among the prisoners who had arrived there the previous year: two executions, one accidental drowning, and the rest mainly from dysentery and malnutrition.

'We had a Union Jack which we'd brought with us from Singapore. When a POW died, a coffin would be built hurriedly for him on the camp and the flag would be draped over it. A party of six of us would go to the local cemetery, dig the grave and carry out the burial. Padre Todd would go. The funerals were in a designated part of the cemetery – the same area where Tucker and Wade had been executed and buried.

There'd always be an awful atmosphere on the camp whenever one of our men had died. But, with the exceptions of Tucker and Wade, we were at least allowed to give these people decent burials and use the Union Jack.

That changed completely after Saigon.'

◆

It was June 1943.

The prisoners were told that seven hundred fit men – about two-thirds of the camp – had to leave. Ben was among those selected to go, and so was his friend Jack Bunston. Colonel Hugonin would be joining them as their commanding officer, accompanied by his adjutant Captain Faraday.

None of them knew where they were being sent, but the specific need for the seven hundred *fittest* men seemed ominous.

'We hadn't much liked our time in Saigon – the endless hours on the docks, the beatings, the constant hunger. But at least we knew what it involved and we had some kind of a routine.

Now all we knew was that something else lay ahead of us, and we didn't know what it was.

We said our goodbyes to our friends who were staying – that wasn't easy. Then we headed off.'

They collected their few remaining belongings, and marched onto the docks for the final time. From the quayside the men crowded into three heaving riverboats, crammed with more than twice the number of passengers they were licensed to carry.

They sailed for two suffocating days, on short rations, into Cambodia[9]. There the exhausted prisoners disembarked at Phnom Penh, and were led towards the railway station on foot.

They trailed through the streets of Phnom Penh, disorientated and dishevelled. Each of the former Saigon dockworkers was now down to his last pair of shorts and his final tattered shirt:

'The locals looked at us in disbelief as we passed through the town. They were used to seeing white people as being in control, not paraded as underdogs – hungry, worn-out, bedraggled.'

At the station the men were herded into baking-hot closed goods trucks. After a short delay the train moved off, dragging the caged prisoners along like cargo: tightly packed into airless carriages, with no idea where they were going – or why.

As the journey rumbled on into the night, the men took turns to sit on the floors; with the trucks so crowded, most had to stand. The stifling heat and crushing fatigue became intolerable.

The prisoners were too achingly ravenous to think about what kind of ordeal might be awaiting them at their destination:

'We had men in our truck from Welsh mining villages. The hunger and deprivation brought back memories for them of the bad times at the pits – memories of jobless coal miners standing outside the pitheads, singing their Welsh hymns and psalms.

They began to sing **Bread of Heaven** *– "Feed me till I want no more." They sang those words with such feeling. Even today, whenever I hear* **Bread of Heaven***, I think of that journey.'*

---

[9] Also in French Indo-China, and so under Japanese influence (map on page 20).

During the night, the train crossed the border into a new country: Thailand.

At daybreak the train stopped and the men were allowed off for some rice and water. The steam train filled up with water too, and then they returned to their closed-in trucks.

They continued towards Bangkok, where there was another brief stop, and then on to a place called Nong Pladuk. The agonising rail journey – interrupted by just two short breaks for food – had taken thirty-six hours.

The prisoners waited at Nong Pladuk for three days. It was just gone midnight when the men were abruptly told that it was time to start moving again.

They marched in darkness to Ban Pong, where they squeezed onto sideless wagons loaded up with rails and sleepers:

'With no sides to the trucks we had the constant danger of falling out, particularly as we were so cramped. None of us dared nod off to sleep: instead we clung on anxiously to the insides – all that night and all the next day.

At one point, I remember our passing a POW burial ground.'

♦

By early evening, they had reached a place called Tarsao.

The men came off the trucks and were marched down a slippery path into a prisoner-of-war camp. This was not to be their new home: they would be staying here only for the night, and would then move on.

But although their time at Tarsao was to be short, what they saw there as they went into the camp was something the men would never forget:

'The very sight of the prisoners at Tarsao horrified us: they were shockingly, dangerously thin.

They wore nothing but loincloths and all their ribs stuck out. They looked to us like walking skeletons.'

The camp consisted largely of makeshift sick huts, erected and held together with bamboo.

Ben and some others went into them. They found in there – as they had feared that they would – friends they had left in Singapore, now desperately ill in this godforsaken place. Some were hardly recognisable.

The friends told them how they had been moved to Thailand months earlier and what had happened to them since. They also spoke of others who had travelled with them and who had died from overwork and malnutrition – young men in their twenties, in perfect health when Ben had last seen them fifteen months earlier.

♦

That evening, more than a week after leaving Saigon, the seven hundred travellers finally learned from the skeleton men what was happening.

The Japanese were using prisoners of war (and anyone else they could lay their hands on) to build a 260-mile railway from central Thailand into the furthest reaches of Burma. All along the route – through virgin tropical jungle – forced labour camps had been set up for that specific purpose, and new ones were being put up all the time. Tarsao was just one of them.

It was obvious that living and working conditions here had been abominable from the outset. Now, with the start of the monsoon season and the work behind schedule, the situation had reached breaking point.

Many of the seven hundred went without food that evening.

They trudged across the rain-sodden camp, towards the bamboo huts where they would be spending the night. On their way, they saw a small gathering of half-naked prisoners in the distance. It was a burial service for the railway's latest victim.

Part Four

The Railway

'One can take a batch of men, put a quarter of them against a wall and shoot them. Or one can send them all into the jungle to be worked, beaten, starved and deprived of medicines.
The first option is more humane.'

British officer
on the Burma Railway

20

Kinsayok Jungle Camp

THAILAND was the only country in South-East Asia never to have been colonised by the West.

The Thai people had been fiercely proud of their independence, but now life had changed: eighteen months ago, Thailand's military dictator had let the Japanese into the country and had formed an uneasy alliance with them.

From Thailand, Japan had invaded adjoining Burma and seized it from the British; now the Allies were fighting back, and the Japanese needed to carry more troops and supplies into Burma.[10]

They sent these into Burma by sea: the more direct route across the mainland from Thailand to Burma was unusable due to the dense, hilly forests and lack of any road system. But at two thousand miles the sea journey was long and tortuous, exposing the Japanese ships to Allied submarines along the way.

That was why Japan wanted a railway running directly from Thailand into deepest Burma – and wanted it fast.

♦

The railway was not a new idea. The British in Burma had explored the possibility long before the war, and after close investigation they had rejected it: the route was barely habitable, and the geographical obstacles were ferocious.

First, there was the terrain: the thick, mountainous jungle and all the rivers that the railway would need to cross along the way.

---

[10] Map on page 20.

Then there was the climate: not just the tropical heat and humidity, but the relentless monsoon season that dominated six months of the year. This was one of the heaviest rainfall areas in the world. When Ben arrived the wet season had just started, with torrential rain turning the earth underfoot into deep, sticky mud; trying to reconstruct the landscape to support a railway in this deluge would be near impossible.

But it was the third difficulty that had proved conclusive: Thai and Burmese labourers could not be persuaded to work in this bleak, forbidding region. It was cut off from food supplies, riddled with disease – malaria, cholera, hookworm – and utterly desolate.

The Japanese had an answer now to the third problem: they would use forced labour. But the other obstacles remained.

The Japanese technicians knew that this was a five-year job, and they had advised Tokyo accordingly. But the decision was taken to build it in a quarter of that timescale: fifteen months.

By the time the seven hundred prisoners from Saigon had reached Thailand, the work was underway. It had started the previous year at each end of the proposed line – the Thai end and the Burmese end – and was gradually moving towards the middle of the route where the two ends would eventually meet.

Thousands of British and Australian prisoners had been drafted in from Changi, as well as many Dutch prisoners from the Dutch East Indies. A still greater number of Malays, Chinese, Tamils, Indians and others had been press-ganged into the work, or duped into it with false promises of a better life.

Yet, even with this vast workforce, the Japanese had set themselves an unattainable deadline and the work was now badly behind schedule. Instead of revising their projections, they brought in more prisoners and resolved to push everyone on the line even harder than before. The men would be forced to make up the lost ground and finish the job within its original timescale – even if that meant driving them to exhaustion.

The seven hundred men left Tarsao the next morning.

They resumed their journey on open trucks, which took them to a river bank where they disembarked and crammed themselves into small barges – about sixty men to a barge. Rolled-up tents were loaded onto the barges with them.

They sailed upriver and by late evening had reached the site of their new camp. It was a place called Kinsayok.

There was already a prisoner-of-war camp at Kinsayok, but this was not it. The existing camp, which later became known to the men as Kinsayok Main Camp, was several miles away.

There was no camp here: just virgin jungle.

It was raining now and pitch dark; with nowhere for the men to sleep, they spent the night on the barges. The two bargees took up a quarter of the available space, while the seven hundred prisoners squeezed into what was left – even more cramped than they had been throughout the day.

It meant another sleepless night with little to eat or drink.

♦

At daybreak the men began to unload the barges and, under the direction of the guards, started to build their camp.

First they had to cut down the thick jungle growth and clear the site – heavy and unfamiliar work, on no sleep and empty stomachs.

When enough space had been cleared, their next priority was to set up a cookhouse. The men had brought with them some large cast iron vats; they built earth surrounds for them, which they moulded so as to leave enough space underneath the vats to light a fire for boiling water. They had brought primitive army field ovens too.

But the cookhouse could not function out in the open, especially during the wet season. So the men constructed a bamboo framework around it, and collected masses of thatch palm from the jungle; then they laid the thatch palm over the bamboo, forming it into a thick roof to keep the rain out.

This crude arrangement – a thatched roof supported by bamboo poles – was to be the standard structure for all camp buildings and huts from now on.

That included the Japanese guardhouse and camp office, which the prisoners were ordered to build next, followed by their own sick huts. They arranged the huts around an open square area that would be used for morning and evening *Tenko*, along similar lines to the camp at Saigon.

Meanwhile, other prisoners built a simple bamboo fence around the outside of the camp whilst others collected rations and brought in water and firewood for the cookhouse. The cookhouse took its water from the river; the men would have to wash themselves, and what was left of their clothes, further downstream.

As darkness fell, the prisoners put up tents for the night.

They dug a ditch around each of them, to catch as much as possible of the inevitable rainfall which – they hoped – would slide down off the sides of the tents.

But there was a problem:

'Our tents had only one layer of fabric. To have any chance of keeping out the rain, we needed two.

We put lots of bamboo on the ground and tried to sleep on that, so that we didn't have to lie in the wet mud.

But nobody slept much. First, rats came into the tent and ran all over our arms and legs – even faces. And then the rains came down.

It just poured straight into the tent. We were drenched.'

Morning came. The camp was nowhere near finished, but the railway could wait no longer. It was time to start work.

21

Embankments

WITH THE ARRIVAL of the wet season, the most ferocious phase of the *'Speedo'* – the Japanese 'big push' to complete the railway at breakneck speed – had begun.

The men were woken each morning at six. They put on their boots (which most of them still had) and whatever was left of their shirts and shorts. They had no hats.

They took their mess tins and water bottles to the cookhouse where they queued for their morning rice, watery stew and some tea – a change from the Saigon procedure, where the food had been brought out to tables outside the huts. They guzzled it down and then lined up for morning *Tenko* before heading off.

The march to their place of work was longer and more precarious than it had been at Saigon. The prisoners would not be returning to the camp to eat, as they had done from the docks; instead they took their mess tins and water bottles with them. Their midday meal, when the time arrived, would be some more rice and a scrap of dried fish.

Noon, however, seemed an eternity away when the prisoners left for work each morning. The camp, needing to be near the river, was more than two miles from the railway and the prisoners had to forge their way through thick, almost impenetrable jungle before they reached the area of the line where they would be working.

Guards walked on either side. Those towards the back spurred the men on with their bamboo sticks at the first sign of straggling; others, at the front, led the way – the prisoners following them uncertainly over the uneven ground below.

Many of the men strained to see ahead, as they traipsed through the monsoon rain and heavy forest in the early morning light.

The most treacherous part was the ravine: it was forty yards deep. Whichever section of the railway the men were led to on a given day, they always had to cross it.

Two long tree trunks, felled by prisoners on arrival, had been placed horizontally across the ravine to be used as bridges. The men walked over them, acutely conscious of the drop below – a terrifying ordeal for many.

◆

Most of the work that had to be done was caused by the jungle terrain.

The railway needed to follow a straight line wherever possible, and the tracks had to be as horizontal as they could be. So the bumpy landscape – hilly in some areas and falling away in others – would need to be reconstructed before any rails could be laid.

This involved two separate types of work: building embankments and making cuttings (or 'hammer-and-tap'). Initially Ben worked on the embankments.

◆

Embankments were needed wherever the landscape dipped below the intended level of the track. The ground in these areas had to be built up, so that a straight railway line could rest on it.

That meant smashing up rocks and digging up ground from the surrounding area, and piling up the debris where it was needed to support the rails. This build-up of land, on which the railway would sit, formed an embankment.

So some prisoners found themselves digging and trying to break up rocks with pickaxes, while others carried earth and rubble over to the embankment areas. Ben preferred to carry, as he was more accustomed to that from his time on the docks – but this was going to be harder.

They were heavy loads of soil and broken rocks, to be shifted over distances of more than a hundred yards at a time. Sometimes he and another prisoner would lug them across on a stretcher, made from two bamboo poles pushed through an empty rice sack; sometimes he would use a large basket to heave the rubble across on his own.

The ground was sodden, and the prisoners felt their feet and ankles sink rapidly into the mud under the weight of the debris – while repeatedly being screamed at to move faster. When they reached the foot of the embankment, they had to haul themselves and their loads to the top, over loose-chipping surfaces that slid downwards beneath the their feet as they fought their way up.

The moment a man had finished moving a stack, he had to fetch the next one: with the *Speedo* underway, completing the railway in an impossibly short space of time was all that seemed to matter. The guards bawled constantly at the prisoners, accompanied by countless wallopings and shouts of 'Speedo!'

It took very little to prompt one of these bashings: just briefly faltering, or a momentary pause or hesitation, was enough. Sometimes it was involuntary: cramp had frozen the prisoner in his tracks, or he could not do as he was told because he could not understand the guard's instructions. The beatings could take any form: open palms, clenched fists, bamboo sticks, stoning, boot-kicking, or being struck with pickaxes or whatever other implements came to hand.

The food rations were similar to those on the docks: three daily meals, each being an undersized portion of rice (sometimes with an even smaller rissole or piece of salty fish, or some thin stew) and three half-pints of tea or boiled water a day:

'The secret – and I know this sounds strange – was not to drink the water. If you didn't drink it, at least you still had it in your bottle and you knew it was there, and that kept you going.

If you drank it, you'd soon get thirsty again. To be thirsty and know that you'd used up your water was the kiss of death.'

The men assembled for their midday rice in a small jungle clearing, unsheltered from the heavy rain and dangerously exposed to the flying fragments from nearby rock explosions. They barely had time to swallow down their small portions before being summoned back to the embankments; two other breaks were allowed during the day, lasting just fifteen minutes each.

Colossal embankments were needed and they had to be built fast – usually in the pouring rain. Every prisoner had to complete a set volume of work before he could return to the camp at the end of the day; shortly before Ben's arrival, these requirements had been doubled to levels that would have been too demanding for skilled, properly fed workmen.

Many of the prisoners routinely had to continue until late at night, and then set off on the tortuous trudge back to the camp in the dark – some of them scarcely able to walk.

As on the docks, there was a system of token pocket money which would only stretch to a few overpriced necessities from the camp shop; but a prisoner's rest day, previously granted after ten consecutive days' work, was not observed here at all.

The men no longer had the docks to 'pong' food from, but the jungle offered some other possibilities: bamboo shoots were safe to eat, as were some other types of roots; bananas too could be found growing in some areas.

Occasionally prisoners would come across a python. They learned how to kill one by bashing its head, and would bring it back to the cookhouse. They also gave the cooks anything else they found that looked edible – rats, lizards, snakes – to add to the stew.

Yet the hunger was always there. The men continued on the same rations that had left them feeling so empty at Saigon, but now with far greater exposure to tropical disease, no sanitation, and – worst of all – the devastating tyranny of the *Speedo*.

– 22 –
Hammer-and-Tap

CUTTINGS had to be made through the rocks and humps of the craggy jungle, to create a level path for the track to run through. This was done in two stages, but it was the first of these – known as 'hammer-and-tap' – that involved practically all of the work.

'Hammer-and-tap' was the long-drawn-out process for the prisoners of drilling three-foot deep holes into the obstructing rocks, using only their bare hands and the most primitive of implements. The holes needed to be in specific places as directed by the Japanese engineers. When eventually the holes were finished, explosives were inserted into them.

Then, the second stage: activating the detonator. The engineers did this, blowing up the part of the rock that had been causing the obstruction.

Some rocks were larger than others, and prisoners worked at different rates. There would be men still drilling their holes when the engineers were ready to blast nearby:

'They often gave us no proper warning, so we didn't have time to get to a place of safety.

All of a sudden, there'd be shards of rock hurtling about us everywhere. Even when the engineers weren't detonating, we had the constant anxiety of not knowing if they'd give us a chance to get out of the way before the next explosion.

There were engineers who found it hilarious – they'd watch us intently with each blast and laugh out loud when we flinched.

But it wasn't funny. It caused some serious injuries.'

In between these sudden panics, the prisoners slaved on. The bawlings and bashings continued, but the men who received the worst of them – stiff from crouching and weak with hunger – could work no faster.

With fraught, tense hands, they struggled for hours to chip away at a stubborn rock. It was harder for some prisoners than for others, and none more so than for Ben.

Kneeling in the granite dust, the men worked in pairs: one to hold a chisel pointing downwards onto the rock, and the other to knock the chisel into it using a fourteen-pound sledgehammer.

Trying to drive a long chisel deep into limestone rock was jarring, backbreaking work. Nobody could bang on the chisel all day long: the two prisoners had to take it in turns.

Ben's problem was that he found himself unable to wield the sledgehammer with any kind of accuracy or control. It was too heavy and too cumbersome:

'I had no experience of anything like this and soon realised that I just wasn't in control of the hammer. I became concerned that I was going to miss the chisel and injure my work partner instead – his hands that were holding the chisel, or his fingers or his wrists or his arms.

Once that thought had entered my head, I found it impossible to think about anything else. So, when it was my turn to use the sledgehammer, I applied it very slowly and gingerly – which was useless, of course, for getting the chisel into the rock.'

This infuriated the guards – they kept screaming 'Speedo!' at him – but there was nothing he could do about it: he could not take the risk of mutilating another prisoner.

It led to frequent beatings throughout the day, mostly with a bamboo stick across his back and shoulders while he toiled on his knees over the chisel.

His final shirt was gone by now.

No prisoner was allowed to return to the camp until he had completed a three-foot deep hole; for Ben and his unfortunate work partner, that could mean very late at night. He was consistently among the last to finish work after a day of hammer-and-tap.

By that time it would be pitch dark. Tracks had been cleared along the route back to the camp, and the two of them had to feel their way down the long, uneven path through the jungle.

At some point, they would know they had reached the ravine with the two trees across it:

'It was a forty yard drop. I couldn't walk along an invisible tree trunk in pitch black, and so I had to get down on all fours to feel where it was.

Then I slowly edged my way forwards and crawled across, clutching onto the trunk with my hands and knees as best I could – just blindly fumbling my way across and hanging on for dear life.'

The tree trunk stretched for yards across the ravine, but that was only part of the problem: it being the monsoon season, the trunk was coated in wet mud from the boots of all the men who had walked on it during the day.

'I needed to get a good grip of the tree to be able to lever myself forwards, but the sludge all over it made that impossible. With the tree being so slippery, I knew how easily I could slide off and fall if I lost my balance.'

Eventually he reached the other side and hoisted himself up onto his feet, to continue groping his way back through the dark – shirtless, muddy, hungry, exhausted and battered – while trying to close his mind to the fact that he would be woken at six tomorrow to do it all again.

It normally happened in the pelting rain.

– 23 –
Health and Safety

TOWARDS the back of the camp, the men had dug themselves 'slit-trench' latrines: long outdoor ditches, for use as toilets.

'They were just open trenches, with no lids or covers. There was nothing out there to sit on, and no shelters or partitions.

We had to squat over these ditches in the monsoon rain, with absolutely no privacy: there'd be lots of us using them all at once, with not much space in between us. At one point we had a bar to hold onto and steady ourselves, but that was all.

The trenches quickly turned into cesspits of reeking filth and crawling maggots. We hated using them, and all the illness on the camp just made it worse. A lot of men found themselves having to rush out to the latrines twenty times a day.'

Throughout the wet season, these open trenches filled up with rain and overflowed, spilling their foul contents over a wide surrounding area. The inevitable result for the prisoners was rampant, persistent dysentery.

Dysentery became the main killer, but there were also all the results of malnutrition – such as avitaminosis, which blurred prisoners' vision. Usually there were no outward symptoms, and the guards refused to believe that anything was wrong.

By contrast, the symptoms of pellagra – blotchy mauve skin patches with dry streaks – were hard to miss; often it affected the prisoner's tongue, so that eating rice became excruciating. Left untreated, pellagra was characterised by 'the four Ds': diarrhoea, dermatitis, dementia and death.

Beriberi, the result of a diet too dependent on polished white rice, attacked the nervous system with unendurable burning and itching sensations, accompanied by huge puffy swellings and an overpowering sense of lethargy and depression.

There had been malnutrition and overwork at Saigon, but the *Speedo* in the rainy season and the jungle squalor of the camp now placed matters on an entirely different scale.

'We were expendable. All that mattered to them was their railway and getting the absolute maximum amount of work out of us each day that they could. They didn't care if we stopped dead in our tracks.'

The seven hundred men – specifically chosen as those who had been the least susceptible to illness at Saigon – were now falling victim to dysentery, malnutrition and exhaustion in numbers that dwarfed anything that had happened on the docks.

♦

With so many sick, the Japanese were left with too few working prisoners to make the progress that the *Speedo* required:

'So the guards started going into the sick huts and demanding that desperately ill men go onto the railway. Some of them close to death.

And when the doctors protested, they beat the doctors up.

We saw it happen every single day: hopelessly sick prisoners dragged out of their huts by their hair and beaten out to work. Just beaten out with sticks. It started very soon after we'd joined the railway and it went on. Our doctors continued to protest, and carried on getting beaten up for it.

There was a Sergeant Okada, of the Japanese medical unit. He placed himself above our doctors and overruled their opinions. They repeatedly made requests to him for medical supplies but he didn't want to know and we never got any.

We knew him as Doctor Death.'

Okada was said to regard a man as fit for work so long as he could stand up. The true position, however, was worse: he sent sick men out on hammer-and-tap jobs, so long as they could kneel.

'It was a long and difficult walk to the railway: some of these men had to be carried, and many died before they got there. If they reached the railway alive, they'd be unable to work and get bashed about for being too slow and – if they survived the working day – they could well die on the way back to camp.'

Sergeant Okada was later tried and convicted as a war criminal. In the meantime, as more prisoners became unable to work, those still on the railway were driven harder and increasingly became sick themselves.

◆

'You'll remember that we'd left Saigon as seven hundred reasonably fit men.'

I did remember that. They had been picked as the fittest two-thirds of the Saigon prisoners.

I could tell that this was leading somewhere: his manner had stiffened and he was speaking very slowly and very deliberately. If he had been a book, he would have said it in bold print:

'We were 700 fit men when we'd left Saigon. But in one month on the railway – in just one month – we lost 140.'

24

The Fence

AFTER an arduous day on the embankments, Ben had managed to make it back to the camp before sunset.

He decided to go down to the river while it was still light, to wash off the sweat and filth of the railway. Ben took the most direct route, which was to walk out through the camp fence (rather than go via the guardhouse, which would mean a detour).

There was nothing unusual about this: prisoners routinely went through the fence to go to and from the river and nobody ever questioned it. The fence, built by the prisoners to Japanese orders, was no more than a skeletal criss-cross framework of bamboo sticks; there were large gaps between them and it was easy to walk straight through.

The fence was not meant to be treated as a prison wall: it was simply there to delineate between the inside of the camp and the outside. The thick surrounding jungle was more than adequate to serve as an escape barrier on its own – which was why other camps in the area had no fence at all.

Having walked through the fence, Ben proceeded towards the river. But he had only gone a few yards when he heard a voice from behind, shouting angrily in Japanese. He assumed, correctly, that this was being directed at him.

He turned around to see a Japanese guard squatting on the ground at the foot of a tree, just off the pathway that had been trodden in for the route down to the river.

'I gave him a bow and then he spoke to me. He wanted to know where I was going, so I indicated the river. Then he just

*had a "whoosh" at me – a smash in the face. I had no idea why,
as I'd bowed to him. Then another whoosh, and then another.*

*Then he pointed at the guardroom, and I understood. He'd
decided that I wasn't allowed to go through the fence.*

*So he beat me up there and then and, when he was finished,
he waved me on to the river. I went down, washed, came back to
the camp and that was that.'*

Being assaulted for practically no reason (and seeing it done
to others) was now such a normal occurrence that Ben had put
the incident behind him by the time evening *Tenko* came around.

It was the usual procedure: the prisoners assembled on the
square and the guards counted them. The headcount confirmed
that nobody had escaped that day, and *Tenko* was almost over.

But first the Japanese officer had an announcement: someone
had gone through the fence and would he step forward.

Ben obeyed. He knew what to expect next:

*'What they'd do would be to start off by talking to you
quietly. Then they'd get a little louder, and then a little louder –
and then the fists would start flying.'*

I could not help noticing his use of the word 'you': he was
talking about what had happened to *him*, but he had seen it done
to others so often that he could speak of it in this impersonal
way. Perhaps also the 'you' helped to distance him in his own
mind from what had happened:

*'They'd be shouting and ranting at the top of their voices and
knocking you about over your head and face.*

*Then, when you were ducking and being pushed about, they'd
go straight for your stomach. Automatically you'd double up
and they'd just keep punching and hitting.*

*Invariably they'd get you floored onto the ground and then
start kicking you bodily.'*

Nobody was shocked. This was unusual only in that it was taking place at *Tenko*, in front of the whole parade.

'By this stage, you'd get three or four of them joining in the fun of kicking you while you were on the ground and bashing you about.
I'd seen it so many times.'

His tone as he said this was entirely matter-of-fact. He had obviously felt pain, but no particular humiliation. Why should he? If any part of the purpose of doing this in front of hundreds of onlookers had been to demean him, then it had not worked.

'Eventually it was over and the parade was dismissed.
A group of our men came over to me to see if I was all right, and then they helped me across to the sick huts.
The doctor checked me over. It was a very nasty beating up and I was badly bruised for days afterwards. But there were no broken bones, and so I was discharged.'

I asked him if that meant he was considered fit enough to return to the railway the following morning.

He answered yes. He seemed surprised that I had even asked.

It had, I suppose, been a stupid question. The guards would obviously never acknowledge that the 'punishment' they had so publicly meted out to him could justify any kind of a respite.

But the key point was simply this: in the context of the *Speedo* and everything else that was going on, a prolonged and violent assault of this kind was practically a non-event. He was a routine case who did not require any special treatment and could go straight back to heavy work as if nothing had happened.

That really brought it home to me. The men in the sick huts – the ones the doctors would take a beating for themselves so as to protect them from the clutches of Sergeant Okada – must have been in a terrible way.

25

Kinsayok Main Camp

THE PRISONERS WORKED on that stretch of the railway for fifteen consecutive days. On the sixteenth day, Ben and five hundred others were marched through the heavy forest to Kinsayok Main Camp. They would build more railway from there.

The men set off after morning *Tenko* and fought their way through the jungle thickets and cloying monsoon mud. They reached their destination by early evening: a larger (but no less overcrowded) camp than the one they had built themselves, and every bit as squalid.

It was situated on a riverbank, in a geological basin which collected and retained all the heavy downpours of the wet season. There was flooding everywhere: the camp was a swamp, thick with the stench of its overflowing latrines.

The layout and foul sanitation arrangements were the same as before. Some work to the camp was needed on the prisoners' arrival but, with Dutch and Javanese prisoners already there, the men did not have to build this time from scratch.

The prisoners slept in tumbledown huts – rotting bamboo shacks with weatherworn palm thatch roofs. At night the men lay on communal platforms (one running along each of the hut's two longest sides), constructed from scores of bamboo sticks fixed together.

The huts were waterlogged in a steadily rising mud pool which lay stagnant across the camp. Mosquitoes, lice and maggots infested the bamboo sleeping platforms, and rain seeped in through the thatching.

On arrival, Colonel Hugonin assumed the same role of dealing with the Japanese commandant and managing the prisoners that he had been performing until now. Since joining the railway he had continued to stand up fearlessly to the Japanese, supported by his adjutant Captain Faraday who had grown to detest them.

Responsibilities changed, however, with the arrival of a substantial British and Australian party. Their commanding officer was a Colonel Lilly, who took over from Colonel Hugonin as the officer with overall charge of the camp's prisoners and became their main spokesman in dealings with the Japanese commandant. Hugonin meanwhile continued to play a pivotal role in representing the large contingent who had travelled with him from Saigon.

At the same time, Captain Faraday stood down as camp adjutant. He had loathed his captors from an early stage, and had long since ceased to make any secret of the fact.

Faraday's replacement as adjutant was a member of his own regiment, a Captain MacDonald:

'As adjutant, Captain MacDonald had an extraordinary knack of managing the Japanese who were running the camp: if he didn't like what they said, he'd just laugh at them. Not with them, but at them. Just laugh in their faces.

Don't ask me why, but somehow this clicked – they didn't mind it. Perhaps it was something they hadn't seen before. They were probably more used to seeing everyone quivering in front of them.

He got onto some kind of a wavelength with them that way. Not by kowtowing and scraping – he would never have demeaned himself – but by laughing quite openly in their faces. I got to see it at close quarters later on. It was some kind of magic that he had, and he got away with murder.

He even managed to keep Sergeant Okada from some of his worst excesses.'

Okada's 'worst excesses' included a grotesque form of water torture, inflicted on men for no conceivable purpose. He would also hurl boulders down onto the working prisoners from a mountain top – and spent hours at a time tormenting the doctors.

He made them stand outside to attention for long periods, while he sat scrutinising them from under the shade of a tree; then he would get up and start hard-slapping them around the face and kicking them in the groin, while bellowing manically at them to cut down their sick lists. If he was drunk, he would brandish his sword at them for further effect.

He used a different sword – a wooden one – for beating sick prisoners out to work. That continued every day.

♦

The men began to see Malay workers on the railway. Some of them had been cajoled from their homes with false promises of what to expect; others had been coerced.

Asians – not only Malays but also Tamils, Chinese and Indians – made up three-quarters of the workforce. They had been dragooned here in vast numbers; they had no collective body to speak for them or to hold them together, and no medical support of any kind. Their survival rates were appalling.

It all put paid to the myth of the 'Greater East Asia Co-Prosperity Sphere' – the Japanese pretence that this was a war to create a better world for fellow Asians.

Less than eighteen months earlier, many in Malaya had believed it. Now, however, countless Asians across the occupied territories had endured the brutal reality: everything taken from them, their lives shattered, and their families' hopes trampled on by the ruthlessness of the Japanese war machine – rape, butchery, torture, slavery, forced prostitution and pillage.

Those who had been marched into these jungles as fodder for the railway were now dying in droves. Here at Kinsayok, terminally sick Malay workers were systematically being clubbed to death and their bodies dumped straight onto the embankments – just to build them up faster.

The prisoners' main job at Kinsayok Main Camp was the construction of a large wooden bridge – one of many that were needed along the route, to support the railway across all the rivers and rifts. The bridge was to be two miles away from the trees whose wood was needed to build it, and so the first task was to fell the trees and move them to the site of the bridge.

The men were led into forest areas and told which tree to cut down; invariably the largest were selected. Then they set to work with a crosscut saw until, eventually, the tree crashed down to the ground. Next they cut off all the branches so as to leave just the straight trunk, to be carried to where the bridge was going to be built.

'They were enormous trees – thirty or forty feet high, and still full of sap. So extremely heavy.

It could take twelve of us to hoist the tree up onto our shoulders – an achievement in itself – so that we could carry it.'

But the men were all of different heights; of the twelve who had lifted the tree, there would typically be four whose shoulders were too low down to support it. The engineers would withdraw the four, leaving the remaining eight with an impossible load to carry over a two mile distance through dense undergrowth – with the added difficulty of having to negotiate the tree's constantly shifting centre of gravity as they manoeuvred it up and down the steep inclines.

No stopping was allowed. In true *Speedo* fashion, the exhausted prisoners – their feet inflamed and swollen – were persistently screamed at to carry the tree faster, backed up with beatings in the usual way.

Elephants had been brought to the area to help move the trees, but they showed no enthusiasm for hauling anything too heavy and the engineers seemed wary of them.

*'In spite of that, I remember seeing a publicity photograph
of an elephant roped up to a huge tree trunk, which it appeared
to be dragging along the ground.*

The photo carried a caption:

*"Even the elephants are doing their bit for the Greater East
Asia Co-Prosperity Sphere!"'*

There was other work too, including a substantial rock
cutting. It was bad news for Ben: more hammer-and-tap.

Ben was paired up for work one morning with his friend Guy
Slater. Slater started the day reasonably fit – or as fit as any of
them were by now – and remained so until mid-morning when,
unexpectedly, he let go of the hammer and stopped work.

Slater looked awful. His whole appearance had suddenly
changed: the skin around his face – now pale and ashen –
seemed to have tightened, making his cheeks go hollow and his
eyes bulge. He doubled up, clutching his stomach, and began
quivering uncontrollably. Slater was in agony – and it was
getting worse.

The panic-stricken guards instantly recognised Slater's
symptoms and, backing nervously away from him, ordered that
he immediately be removed from the worksite.

That evening, Slater's corpse was incinerated to stem the
spread of infection. Cholera had arrived at Kinsayok.

◆

Work on the line continued, until the obstructing hills and rocks
had been demolished and large enough embankments had been
built to raise those areas where the ground had been too low.
The terrain was now level enough to take the track, and it was
time to start laying the railway.

First the prisoners had to put down the sleepers – the
rectangular slabs that would form the base of the track. Then
they laid the rails. Once the correct position had been found for
them, the men had to fix them into the sleepers with long spikes
which they knocked into the ground with sledgehammers.

It remained remorselessly hard work, and all the brutalities of the *Speedo* – the constant haranguing, the beatings, the sick men being dragged out of their huts – never loosened their grip.

♦

The docks and the railway had taken their toll on the prisoners' boots. The Japanese authorities refused to replace footwear, and growing numbers of men were walking barefoot over sharp granite chippings and through heavy mud.

The prisoners' shirts in the meantime had long gone, and the patches that made up their shorts were barely holding together.

As their shorts disintegrated, the men replaced them with small loincloths cut out from the remnants of their old shirts. The result was a rectangular piece of cloth, one side of which was extended at either end to form a cord. The cord was tied around the waist, from which the rectangle was passed down and between the legs, and then drawn up again at the other side and tucked under the cord.

It became the standard prisoner uniform: no shirt and no trousers – just a loincloth. Ben was among the many who had no hat; he still had his army boots, but they were rapidly coming apart.

The men had grown dangerously thin. As they went about in their loincloths, all their ribs protruded and practically all of the prisoners displayed prominent bruises and lesions.

In almost no time, they had turned into the skeleton men they had seen at Tarsao.

26

Rice Sacks

THE THIN LOINCLOTHS provided no protection, leaving the near-naked prisoners hopelessly exposed to the pounding down of the heavy rains, bug bites of every kind, and all the scratches and scrapes of the dense tropical jungle.

The area most at risk was below the knees:

'We had to be particularly careful whenever we walked near bamboo shoots. If the shoots caught us on our legs or ankles and gashed the skin, matters could very quickly turn nasty.'

Seemingly trivial nicks and cuts would not heal for the lack of nutrition, and rapidly became infected in the abject jungle filth of the camp. They developed into open sores:

'The sores turned into ulcers which ate away, deeper and deeper, into the flesh.'

Tropical ulcers appeared on both of Ben's shins in this way.

In his kit bag he had a tiny tube of sulpha; he had 'ponged' it from the docks in Saigon. He had thought at the time (correctly, as matters turned out) that it probably took its name from the sulphonamide anti-bacterial drugs which had been marketed in Britain before the war.

When his ulcers started, he applied the sulpha to them; the sulpha was in the form of a paste, which smarted as he rubbed it onto the raw lesions. It was only a small tube and it did not go far – but it was enough: his ulcers healed.

Others were unluckier. In the space of two days, a routine scratch could turn into a gaping, life-threatening leg wound – bone exposed and oozing pus.

A designated ulcer hut was set up for these, well away from the other prisoners because of the stench of the rotting flesh:

'The ulcers were horribly painful, and treating them caused agony. Just trying to keep the wound clean – scraping it out from the inside with a teaspoon – was excruciating.

There were a lot of men who could only be saved by amputation. Unfortunately, that became very commonplace.

Normally one leg. Sometimes both.'

The amputations were carried out above the knee, and had to be performed with the crudest of tools: a cut-throat razor, a carpenter's saw, and domestic needle and thread.

And no anaesthetics.

◆

Immense responsibility fell on the camp's medical officers. One of these was the legendary 'Weary' Dunlop, the Australian surgeon whose courage and selflessness seemed almost superhuman; another was Stanley Pavillard, a larger-than-life character who was known for having conducted his daily patient rounds on a stretcher when he had been ill himself.

They and their orderlies battled against the most unforgiving odds: guards undermining their every move, persistent beatings for protecting the sick, practically no resources, and their own susceptibility to hunger and illness like anyone else.

◆

Growing numbers of men had reached a point where they could not face any further rice. Sometimes this was a known symptom of pellagra, but often the prisoner could simply stand no more.

One of the medical officers had some particularly direct advice for these men: 'It's rice or rice sacks.'

Every prisoner knew what that meant: the camp's dead were bundled into rice sacks for burial. (Coffins could no longer be built as they had been at Saigon – too many deaths, too little time.) The camp had its own burial ground at the far end, with crosses showing the names of the prisoners buried there.

But there were no burials for the cholera victims: they were too infectious. Instead their bodies were heaped onto a funeral pyre.

Slater, who fell ill and was cremated on the same day, was typical of the speed and ferocity with which it attacked.

The cholera outbreak struck fear into the hearts of guards and prisoners alike. It was a waterborne disease which thrived in the tropical rivers and monsoon rains. With the overcrowding on the camp and the constant flooding, it spread as rapidly as it killed: agonising gripping pains, profuse vomiting, urgent passing of blood and mucus – it was a savage, horrifying way to die.

'It was so lethal, and so contagious, that a separate cholera hut was set up in the jungle half a mile from the camp.

The guards kept well away – they were terrified of cholera – but there were volunteers among the POWs who bravely went into the hut and did whatever they could to help.

The patients needed saline injections, which had to be administered through a drip. The problem was that there weren't any needles, so they found a way to use bamboo instead. They'd pierce a channel through a bamboo shoot and then slant one end of it, shaping the tip into a sharp point that they could dig into the patient.

They saved a good number, but in the end there were just too many. Most of them died. We lost a lot that way.'

◆

The medical officer's advice – 'It's rice or rice sacks' – was deliberately blunt. Prisoners acted on it, but not always in the way that had been intended.

Some opted for rice sacks. They had had enough.

27

Night

Rᴵᴄᴇ sᴀᴄᴋs were used for another purpose too: bedclothes.

Even here, the nights could be cold – and particularly so for such exhausted, malnourished men. The prisoners pulled empty rice sacks over themselves when they lay down at night, and many used them as sleeping bags:

'The platforms that we slept on – our 'bed slats' – were assembled from strips of bamboo. Just lots of individual bamboo sticks placed side by side and joined together.

So the platforms were hard and uneven, with bumps and ridges everywhere. With our bones sticking out, they hurt to lie on with our bare skin – and so we slept with the rice sack cloth all around us.'

The hessian rice sacks were coarse and abrasive, but less uncomfortable than lying directly on the bamboo platforms. The sacks gave no protection from the swarms of bugs and mosquitoes that infested the bed slats: they crawled all over, into the rice sacks and everywhere else.

The platforms were packed. There was no space between the prisoners to let them move or turn over when they were restless, and rain from the heavy downpours came through into the hut during the night.

Even so, Ben did not have much difficulty in falling asleep at the end of the day; it was usually gone midnight, and the men had been driven relentlessly since dawn. But it was a tense, frenetic sleep, haunted by recurring images of the day's ordeal.

The hut would periodically be disturbed by an anguished scream or outburst: nightmares normally forgotten by morning.

Prisoners racked with perpetual dysentery woke repeatedly during the night, urgently needing the latrines. They headed out into the torrential rain, and scrambled barefoot through the dark – over mud, faeces and maggots – in a desperate dash for the fetid open trenches. A detestable business even by day.

At six in the morning the bugle sounded: for those who had survived the night, the railway beckoned. They felt as if they had only just lain down.

◆

All along the railway, there were men who kept diaries and drew sketches of what they experienced and saw. They used whatever scraps of cardboard or paper they could find: the blank unprinted margins torn from books, or even toilet paper stolen from the guards (the prisoners having none of their own).

Some of them buried their notes or drawings in the ground beneath their bed slats; others would fold them up until they were small enough to fit into tiny hollow spaces in the bamboo, or squeeze them into the thatched roofs.

Some even hid them in the cholera huts where the guards were afraid to go, or buried them in the graves of their lost friends, hoping – one day – to return and retrieve them.

Louis Baume, also then at Kinsayok, kept a diary on pieces of tissue paper. He wrote during the *Speedo* there:

I have been working on the stone cutting, by far the worst job now, an absolute hell under the swinish Nips. The tasks on the earth cutting and the stone cutting have been doubled to two cubic metres per man! It's well nigh impossible. The working conditions are almost unbearable – hacking away at the rock in the full glaze of the midday sun or digging up the thick red clay and mud in teeming rain: bare-footed, with feet cut and bleeding from the broken rock or sharp bamboo thorns, hatless and naked except for a brief 'jap-happy'[11]. Most of our clothes are worn out and rotten and only a few of us have hats, shorts or footwear. And all the time the blasted, bloody Nips screaming and shouting, bellowing, beating, bashing, kurrahing[12], kicking and hurling stones, sticks and insults, forever urging, forcing and bullying us to work faster, faster and faster. And at the end of the long day's work we stumble back to camp in the dark, along a rutted road knee-deep in thick black jungle mud. And after a poor and insufficient supper eaten in the pitch dark or, at the most, by the dim light of flickering coconut-oil lamp filling the foul air with its thick black smoke, we lie down to sleep on the bamboo slats of our filthy hut, crawling with bed-bugs, lice and maggots. It is a restless sleep for even then we are carried back to the green and dripping jungle to carry fantastic loads of eternal bamboo or baskets of earth while all the yellow devils of Hell stand around with sticks in their hands, shouting and kurrahing us on to work faster, faster, faster. And in the morning it all starts over again. There is no end to all this – except one – it just seems to go on and on.

---

[11] Loincloth. Some prisoners called their loincloths 'Jap-happies', because they resembled what the Japanese guards wore as underwear.

[12] 'Kurrah!' – when shouted angrily at a prisoner – was an aggressive and threatening demand for his attention. It was normally followed by some act of violence against him.

Part Five

The Prisoner List

'Death walked among us so freely that it came to have little significance. The forests of crosses show the countless, needless deaths – whether the civilised world will call them by some stronger name remains to be seen.'

British commanding officer
shortly after completion of the railway

– 28 –
Trench Foot

AFTER ONE MONTH on the railway, the work at Kinsayok was complete.

For the seven hundred men who had arrived in June, the impact had been devastating. Even the Japanese, whose sole concern remained the completion of the railway, could only pronounce a quarter of that group who had endured the *Speedo* as capable of any further railway work at all.

These were moved to another railway camp, Krian Krai. Meanwhile the group's medical officer – his pleas for essential medicines still being denied – received a particularly ferocious punishment beating for the high sick rate.

Ben was among the remaining three-quarters who stayed at Kinsayok. One in every four of these was capable of extremely light work; all the others – more than half of the seven hundred considered fit a month earlier – were unfit for anything.

Well over a third of this huge last group (or one in five of the seven hundred 'fit') were now at death's door – and would be dead in the coming days, weeks and months – or had died already.

Others would live, but would never be themselves again.

♦

It was just as well for Ben that the *Speedo* was over, as he was no longer able to walk. Had the *Speedo* continued, he would have had to be carried to the railway for hammer-and-tap work: he could do that on his knees.

His problem was one more widely associated with soldiers in the First World War: trench foot.

His army boots had survived to the end of the *Speedo* – but only just. The unremitting pressure to keep trudging faster and faster through the squelching mud had loosened the stitching of his boots; the sludge had clung onto each boot as he had dragged one foot after the other out of the mire, progressively pulling the soles away from the uppers. Soaking wet mud had seeped in through the gaps and surrounded his feet, filling the spaces between his toes as he walked.

Soon after the *Speedo*, the boots finally fell apart. His feet had become increasingly sore, and now he could see why: he had been traipsing around in boots filled with thick, congealing mud which had caked around his feet and slowly been tearing away at them. He had lost all of the skin from the upper surfaces of both feet.

With no boots, and with the camp still sodden, he could now bear weight only on his heels:

'The doctor's advice was to get hold of some rags – just remains of old clothing – and then to go to the cookhouse and ask them for some fat of some sort. I had to put the fat on my feet and toes, and then soak the rags in the fat and wind them around my feet.

After that I just had to make sure I kept my feet out of the mud.'

Ben followed the advice and waited patiently for his skin to heal.

He used two bamboo sticks to steady himself and to help lever himself forwards as he moved with difficulty around the camp. Only his heels touched the ground, with the rest of his feet pointing upwards. If anyone looked like coming too close, he would lift one of the sticks so that they stayed away from his raw feet.

Captain MacDonald came across Ben hobbling around in this awkward manner, trying to keep his feet out of the mud. Captain MacDonald was the camp adjutant.

'"You're in a right mess," he said cheerily, when he saw me. "You'd better come into the office. There's work in there that you can do sitting down, and at least you'll be dry."'

There were two men working in the camp office in addition to Captain MacDonald; the camp still had hundreds of prisoners (mostly sick) and so there was certainly work to be done. Captain MacDonald explained to Ben how the office operated and gave him some general routine tasks.

♦

Ben was surprised to discover that the office had no list of the thousand men of 'Saigon Battalion' who had sailed from Singapore to Saigon nearly eighteen months earlier.

A full list had been passed to Sparks soon after reaching Saigon, but there was no list now and the reason for that was unknown. Perhaps Sparks had been given the only list that there was, although that seemed unlikely. Probably there was a list still on the camp in Saigon – but it was of no use there for the seven hundred who had since moved to Thailand.

Ben mentioned the point to Captain MacDonald who, as one of Saigon Battalion himself, shared Ben's concern. It was, he agreed, a serious problem. Now that the *Speedo* was over, they ought to have a record of who was where and – in an increasing number of cases – what had happened to them.

It was more than just a matter of principle. One day the information might be required for war crimes investigations; it might also be needed to inform parents of what had happened to their sons. But there were other reasons too: if the prisoners should ever be lucky enough to meet somebody like Sparks again, he would need the list to be able to smuggle the information back home – as Sparks had done.

When Ben returned to the camp office the next morning, Captain MacDonald had obtained from somewhere (Ben did not know where) a blank writing book – small, lined and inexpensively bound – so that Ben could start to compile a list of names.

◆

Kinsayok was now a camp of mainly sick and dying men.

The place was in a strange kind of limbo, where little happened and the prevailing mood was one of stunned bewilderment at the barbarity that had taken place there. In the shadow of the *Speedo* came delayed shock and the worsening, abject misery of its victims.

The medical officers had their successes, but growing numbers of men were beyond rescue. Some tropical ulcers slowly improved; others continued to rot away at the flesh, leaving no alternative to amputation. Some of the sickest men started to regain their strength and even became fit for light work; others edged closer to death each day. Some clung resolutely to life, determined to return to the way they had been only a few weeks earlier – often in vain; others just lay there, their eyes unfocused, in bleak, hopeless silence.

The Japanese ordered that a large number from the sick huts be transferred back to Tarsao, which had now been designated a hospital camp; others were to be sent to another hospital camp, called Chungkai.

These were not hospitals: just collections of sick huts on a larger scale than those at Kinsayok. The stretch of track from Kinsayok to the hospital camps had been completed, and so the sick prisoners were to make their journey along the railway that had brought them to this sorry state.

Before they were bundled onto the trucks, the guards forcibly removed the men's army boots and kept them.

Sick men did not need boots, they said.

29

The Record Book

WITH MANY of the sickest prisoners leaving the camp and others slowly regaining their strength, an increasing proportion of those remaining at Kinsayok found that they could do some form of light work.

They were mostly given undemanding jobs, such as going about the camp with a broom just to help keep them active.

Others built underarm crutches for the amputees. Later, they developed more advanced skills and began to make artificial limbs using wood and whatever items of leather they could find on the camp.

Some, as they grew stronger, began to return to the railway to perform small maintenance jobs which involved nothing like the intensity of the *Speedo*.

Ben, with his trench foot, continued to work in the camp office.

As his feet became less painful, Ben began to move around the camp more and started to seek out the various sergeant-majors.

Captain MacDonald had explained to him that each sergeant-major in Saigon Battalion would have had a list of the men in his particular unit. If Ben could obtain all of those lists, he would have the raw material that he needed for his record book.

The difficulty was in locating the sergeant-majors. Those who were still at Kinsayok were happy to lend Ben their lists, but there were sergeant-majors who had been transferred to other camps. These had either provided a copy of their lists to another sergeant-major or left a sergeant beneath them who had his own copy; the problem was finding the right person. After much ferreting, however, Ben had all the lists that he needed. Taken together, the names on the lists covered not only the seven hundred men sent to Thailand, but also the others who had stayed at Saigon – so encompassing the full thousand men of Saigon Battalion.

Transcribing a thousand names legibly into one consolidated volume took some time. He had only a small book to write them in, with no spare paper or other notebook if he made a mistake. To fit the information in, he wrote in tiny, but very clear, block capitals. Great care was needed: there was no space for crossings out and manual corrections.

He divided each left-hand page into columns, where he listed the thousand men by name, age, occupation, rank, army number and prisoner number. On the facing right-hand page, he inserted whatever other information was available – such as next of kin, any other relevant family information and home address. For the men who had not been sent to Thailand – about one in every three – he wrote in that they had remained in Saigon.

Some of those named on the sergeant-majors' lists were shown as having died; Ben already knew about many of these – particularly those that had occurred at Saigon, where the death of a prisoner had been comparatively rare (although it had not seemed so at the time). He underlined these names in red in his book and noted the cause, place and date of death on the right-hand page. Prisoners also came to him to confirm the details of more recent deaths at Kinsayok – vastly more had resulted from one month of the *Speedo* than had occurred in fifteen months at Saigon – and he noted those too.

He returned the lists to the sergeants and sergeant-majors. By now, his feet had improved and he was able to go to the burial ground at the far end of the camp. He checked its layout, the positions of the graves and the names on the crosses. Then he went back to the office and drew a plan of it at the back of the book, numbering the plots where Saigon Battalion prisoners were buried and referencing those numbers in the list alongside the deceased prisoners' names. He also included details of coastal observation detachments (radar groups), in addition to the thousand men of Saigon Battalion.

The book was now as up-to-date as it could be with the available information. It was not complete, however, primarily because of the prisoners who had been moved to the two hospital camps after the *Speedo*; they had included many of the sickest men on the camp, and it was inevitable that some of these must have died since leaving.

The death toll at Kinsayok meanwhile continued to grow.

The Japanese interpreter frequently dropped into the Allies' office without warning. His aim was to find out what they were doing and to inspect whatever papers or documents they had. He would be looking for anything he could hit upon that could be regarded in any way as anti-Japanese.

Ben's record book certainly fell into that category. It had started only as a list of the men in his contingent; the compiling of such a list was itself a prohibited activity, but it had now grown into something much more serious. The interpreter would undoubtedly regard the book – particularly with its plan of the camp cemetery and the many underlined names indicating deaths from overwork, malnutrition and the refusal of medical supplies – as anti-Japanese propaganda; if the book were ever to be smuggled out of the camp (perhaps through sympathetic Thai traders who delivered to the camp shop), it could result in far more interest being taken in the outside world about the treatment of prisoners by the Japanese.

So the book was kept well hidden. When Ben was working on it, he had to be ready at all times to conceal it at a moment's notice; the same applied to Captain MacDonald and to anyone else in the camp office who had cause to refer to it.

Then, late one afternoon, the Japanese interpreter wandered breezily into the office, clearly having had too much to drink. It had happened before, and so Ben and the others who were there knew that this presented them with an opportunity.

As on previous occasions, the interpreter was holding his rubber stamp. The stamp was his seal of approval: any document or book which bore the stamp's mark was deemed to have been examined and sanctioned by him. This made the stamp a symbol of his status and of his authority. It was his particular means, as interpreter, of exerting whatever influence he had.

In his drunken state, he was more inclined to use the stamp than he normally would have been. It was hard to tell why: it may just have been a more relaxed and magnanimous frame of mind brought on by the drink; it may also have been that – when drunk – using the stamp gave him the feeling that he was somehow wielding the power of his position.

Ben and the other two men who were in the office sat him down and placed some entirely uncontroversial papers in front of him. As they had hoped, he stamped them after little more than a cursory glance. Then they presented some other papers, and then some more, until he was in the rhythm of stamping whatever they put there without his even looking at it.

The next item was the record book. He stamped that too.

A few minutes later he was gone.

30

Wish You Were Here

IN THREE AND A HALF YEARS as a prisoner, Ben received five deliveries of post and had a similar number of opportunities to write home.[13] The Geneva Convention envisaged that these should have been monthly (forty-two), at the absolute least.

The messages home had to be in a standard form, for which the prisoners were given pre-printed postcards. The cards looked something like this:[14]

IMPERIAL JAPANESE ARMY

I am interned in ....

My health is excellent.
I am ill in hospital.

I am working for pay.
I am not working.

My best regards to ....

                           Yours ever ....

---

[13] For many prisoners it was worse. Just three deliveries and three communications home (and in many cases fewer) was normal.

[14] There were two main forms of postcard: this is an amalgam of the two. The version provided at Saigon did not permit the prisoner to state his location.

Forced to choose between the extremes of 'My health is
excellent' and 'I am ill in hospital', practically all of the
prisoners – even the worst of the sick hut cases – opted for 'My
health is excellent'.

Prisoners also selected 'working for pay' over 'not working'.
The truth – 'I am working for virtually no pay' – did not appear
on the form.

The cards were heavily vetted before they were sent. The
prisoners were allowed to fill in the blanks, but no more; in
particular, they were not permitted to give the date.

It was at this time that Ben sent the second of his cards home;
the first had been shortly before leaving Saigon.

On this occasion, he completed the final line so that it read:
'My best regards to Ross and Shona Shani.'

It was Sam, Ben's teenage brother, who deciphered the
message: if 'Ross and Shona' is said quickly enough, it sounds
like *Rosh Hashanah. Rosh Hashanah* is the Jewish New Year,
and *Shani* is Hebrew for 'two'.

Ben was telling them that he had still been alive during the
second Jewish New Year since they had last seen him.

♦

The family had received one letter from the War Office and two
postcards from Ben since he had been taken prisoner.

But Mrs Youle – also in Edgware – had received no news at
all of her son in that time.

Ben's mother tried to dissuade her from losing heart, but it
was too late for that now. Mrs Youle had been absolutely
certain, ever since before the fall of Singapore, that he was dead.

Although she was correct, her reasoning was based on
nothing more than superstition. (Second Lieutenant Youle, you
will remember, had been killed on Friday the Thirteenth.)

– 31 –
Completion

IN OCTOBER 1943, the two ends of the railway on which work had started the previous year – the Thailand end and the Burma end – met in the middle, close to the border between those two countries. There was now a continuous length of track covering the entire route and the railway was ready for use.

The Japanese had beaten their own impossible target. It was all down to the ferocity of the *Speedo*: the work had been badly behind schedule when the men had arrived in June.

There would always be continuing maintenance work, and parts of the line required improvement. But the railway was there and the constant, screaming urgency of the work – not just at Kinsayok, but all along the line – was over.

That was a relief, but only a qualified one: men were still dying in large numbers and the prisoners increasingly wondered what, if anything, the Japanese planned to do with them next.

Was there another job looming – perhaps as bad as the one that they had just finished? If not, what further use did the Japanese have for them?

The food rations had become even sparser now, and it was obvious from the increasingly filthy state of the rice that there were severe food shortages. With an expanding and increasingly scattered army of their own to feed, how long would it take the Japanese to conclude that the prisoners had outlived their usefulness?

Or had they already decided?

In the meantime, the *Speedo* had achieved exactly what the enemy had wanted: direct access into Burma. Some prisoners felt physically ill when they saw the first trucks travelling through Kinsayok to take men, armaments and supplies into the Burmese jungle to confront the Allies.

The only hope was that the railway would be destroyed by Allied aircraft. But no prisoner relished the prospect of having to rebuild it afterwards – or of being in the area when the bombs came down.

♦

The railway was also used to take prisoners to their places of work (typically to a part of the line that required maintenance), and to move them between camps when it was time for them to relocate from one camp to another.

Prisoners would learn that they were to be transferred to a new camp at a moment's notice. There could be any number of reasons for it: sometimes it was because a particular area of the railway required more maintenance and improvement work; sometimes it was part of the process of concentrating sick prisoners into the hospital camps at Tarsao and Chungkai, or of consolidating larger numbers of prisoners into fewer camps so that the smaller camps could be wound down. Often there seemed to be no reason.

The trains carrying these men along the line routinely went through Kinsayok. If a train or a barge carrying prisoners stopped at Kinsayok for food or water, a group from the camp would go to see if any of the passengers had news of men from Saigon Battalion.

If there was any news, it was likely to be bad: another death from beriberi at Tarsao, or from dysentery at Chungkai.

Once the men had moved on, the Kinsayok prisoners who had spoken to them would relay any information to Ben for the record book.

♦

Of all the prisoners who passed through Kinsayok, it was those of 'F' Force and 'H' Force who had suffered the most:

'There were desperately sick POWs all along the line, but this was truly awful. I remember the remnants of 'F' Force and 'H' Force stopping off at Kinsayok. The condition that they were in when we saw them ... it was just unspeakable.'

A momentary flash of anger swept across his face as he began to tell me how 'F' Force had been duped from the start.

'F' Force was largely made up of men who were sick before they had even left Singapore; that was why they were still there after most of the prisoners had been transferred to Thailand.

Their story started when the Japanese announced the need for seven thousand men to transfer from Changi to a new location. It was not, they emphasised, a work party: it was simply a means of alleviating the food shortages in Singapore.

There would be no work, they were told, and very little marching. It would be an opportunity for the sick to recover in pleasant countryside surroundings with good food and recreational comforts. There would be transport for those unable to walk the short distances involved. It was even suggested that they might like to bring a grand piano with them – and they did.

So they set off on the first leg of their adventure: five punishing days crammed into scorching hot steel rice trucks.

When they came off at Ban Pong, the exhausted men assumed that they had arrived. The guards laughed scornfully: they had a 185-mile march ahead of them. There followed a kit inspection, at which the guards stole whatever they wanted while the prisoners watched. Then the march began.

Soon the men were selling their boots and clothes to the local Thais for food, and dumping other essential belongings. For seventeen days, they were savagely goaded through the muddy terrain and thick, mountainous forest; stragglers were struck with metal clubs. There was no let-up: just short night stops in jungle clearings and staging camps rampant with cholera.

By the time they reached their destination near the Burmese border, hundreds had died by the wayside and many more were having to be carried. But this was the *Speedo*, and sick men were forced to work.

At Songkurai, that meant fifteen-hour days in the monsoon rains with only minutes for 'lunch' – starvation rations, literally. Some had to build a three-span wooden trestle bridge; for this they were made to carry massive logs through knee-deep mud, and work waist-high in freezing cold, rushing river water.

When the work fell behind schedule, they were thrashed with barbed wire. Cholera struck again with devastating force and dysentery was rife.

Now, the line was completed. Those of 'F' Force still alive were squeezed into barges and railway trucks bound for Singapore.

Some stopped at Kinsayok for food. Emaciated like sticks, they had been packed upright into their travel compartments, propped up for support against each other. Most were still vertical, but they were not standing: they did not have the strength to support the little remaining weight of their own shrunken bodies. They had to be gingerly manoeuvred out and carried – many of them practically dead.

♦

Meanwhile, the Japanese had ordered their healthiest-looking prisoners to attend a formal event to mark the opening of the railway. They gave them new uniforms, in which they were filmed laying the last rails; as soon as they were out of camera shot, they had to remove the uniforms and return them.

The Japanese were intent that the world should believe the railway had been built by a happy, well-treated workforce. Prisoners who had compiled evidence to the contrary – diaries, sketches, or records of the kind assembled by Ben – were at risk.

However, eyewitness reports of the true state of affairs were already filtering through to the West.

32

Excellent Barbers

IN JANUARY 1944, the British Foreign Secretary, Anthony Eden, read out a formal statement to the House of Commons:

> I fear I have grave news to give to the House.

> Members will be aware that a large number of postcards and letters have recently been received in this country from prisoners in the Far East and that these almost uniformly suggest that the writers are being treated well and are in good health. I regret to have to tell the House that information which has been reaching His Majesty's Government no longer leaves room for any doubt that the true state of affairs is a very different one so far as the great majority of prisoners in Japanese hands is concerned.

> For some time past, information has been reaching His Majesty's Government regarding the conditions under which prisoners are detained and worked in some of these areas, and as it was of so grave a character as to be likely to cause distress to relatives of prisoners and civilian internees in Japanese hands His Majesty's Government felt bound to satisfy themselves that it was authentic before making it public.

> We are now so satisfied, and it becomes my painful duty to tell the House that in Siam[15] there are many thousands of prisoners from

---

[15] Thailand was still normally referred to as Siam at this time, in spite of the recent name change – see page xii (under the heading *Siam/Thailand*).

the British Commonwealth, including India, who are being compelled by the Japanese military to live in tropical jungle conditions without adequate shelter, clothing, food, or medical attention; and these men are forced to work on building a railway and making roads. Our information is that their health is rapidly deteriorating, that a high percentage are seriously ill, and that there have been some thousands of deaths.

One eyewitness reports of a camp in Siam that 'I saw many prisoners clearly. They were skin and bone, unshaven and with long matted hair. They were half naked.' The same witness reported that they wore no hats or shoes; and this, may I remind the House, in a tropical climate, where the neighbouring country is virtually uninhabited, so that there are practically no local resources which could provide medical or other material relief.

This statement – a shattering blow for the waiting families – was deliberately timed to coincide with similar announcements being delivered in other countries that day. The desperate hope was that world opinion just might influence the Japanese.

And it did – for about two months.

For the first time, the prisoners received a modest issue of clothes; for most of them, this consisted mainly of a new loincloth and some rudimentary footwear. The loincloths were useful, as most prisoners' existing ones – cut out from the remains of their old shirts – were now wearing thin; the new shoes were also worth having, although the many who had been forced to toil barefoot throughout the *Speedo* found it difficult to be grateful.

The shoes were basic: a wooden sole for each foot, with a strip of rubber across to hold it on. They were uncomfortable to walk in and rubbed in places, but for Ben – with his feet now healed – they were invaluable.

There were other improvements too, at least at Kinsayok. The camp authorities became more willing to accept the recommendations of the Allied medical officers, leading to some basic hygiene measures and inoculations for prisoners; there was no improvement in medicines and resources for the existing sick, but at least it was something.

The Japanese commandant asked that a handful of the men should be chosen to write essays for radio broadcast, about their experiences as prisoners since coming to Thailand. It was part of a plan to counteract the recent bad publicity. Colonel Hugonin nominated Ben to compose one of these.

Ben wrote it in the camp office, using a typewriter brought from Singapore; paper was provided. He typed it onto six pages, which he pinned together in one corner using a tiny sliver of bamboo. Then he handed it in for the Japanese interpreter. (The full essay appears in the Appendix from page 207.)

He knew that what he had written would never be broadcast, and that the best he could hope for was not to be beaten too severely for having written it. In this case, his best hopes were exceeded: the essay was returned to him without comment.

Only one of the essays was broadcast. It was Captain Faraday's, and it started roughly like this:

I had never had the pleasure or otherwise of meeting Japanese people until I was posted to Singapore. There I discovered that they were the most excellent barbers – and first-class photographers too.

These were thinly veiled references to the activities of fifth columnists before the invasion. Many Japanese people had been working on the island as photographers, giving them ample opportunity to take copious pictures in and around Singapore without arousing suspicion. Others, working as barbers, had gathered detailed information through seemingly idle chit-chat with local customers while cutting their hair.

The rest of Faraday's essay continued in this vein: damning his captors with faint praise, while wholly avoiding the subject of his experiences as a prisoner of war.

They seemed happy with it.

33

The Betel Nut Women

THE RATIONS had deteriorated – and not only the quantities:

'We were certain by now that we were getting the sweepings from the warehouse floor: rice that had escaped from torn sacks or just been spilt. It must have been lying on the ground for a while before it got to us.

There were weevils in it – bigger than ants, but still small enough to make getting them out of the rice very fiddly. We'd had them in the rice before; it had been going on for a while, but now it was getting much worse and it continued for a long, long time. And not just weevils: maggots too. But particularly weevils.

We had no doubt that there was a genuine food shortage. There just wasn't enough, and we were clearly getting the dregs: the guards' rice was much cleaner than ours.

We tried to flick the weevils out at first, but then there got to be so many of these things that we just became hardened to them. We talked ourselves into believing that they were good for us – that they'd give us protein.'

It also became harder to supplement the rice with purchases from the camp shop. With more prisoners having been moved out of Kinsayok – either to the hospital camps or to other railway camps for maintenance work – the numbers remaining there had declined dramatically. Few Thai traders still considered it worth their while to make deliveries.

The guards had other sources of food:

'They got themselves a number of ducks for their own use and kept them in a compound. That way they had their supply of eggs to eat, and an occasional meal of duck.

Duck eggs provided a lot of the nutrition that rice didn't. Our own doctors told us they were probably the best food we could eat, and so we'd made a point of looking out for them in the camp shop – back in the days when the camp shop had stocked them.

We had two or three POWs assigned to looking after the guards' ducks. Occasionally one of them would wring a duck's neck and whip it back to the cookhouse for food. But more often than not the guards would notice that a duck had gone missing, and then the usual bashings would follow.'

Ben continued to work with Captain MacDonald in the camp office; however, now that he could walk again, he was also frequently joining work parties sent onto the railway to bolster the embankments.

From there, the men saw trains carrying supplies along the line into Burma. In the other direction – returning from the fighting – they also started to see trucks bringing back badly wounded Japanese soldiers.

'But none of that told us how the war was going: we remembered how there'd been Japanese casualties in Malaya too, but they'd still beaten us hollow.

We couldn't afford to lose hope, but we knew that whatever had happened to the Japanese soldiers on those trucks was also probably happening to our own troops in Burma – and perhaps much worse.'

Not to lose hope was an achievement in itself. The prisoners had no sense of when this way of life would ever end – or how.

In the meantime, the more relaxed attitude of the guards following the early completion of the railway had largely passed. The atmosphere on the camp and the mood towards Kinsayok's remaining prisoners returned to normal.

Then, one morning at *Tenko*, the prisoners were told that all except a few of them were to be moved to a new camp – a place called Tamuang.

♦

It was several hours' ride along the railway to their new camp.

The men, including the sick, squeezed onto the trucks. They took with them what was left of their belongings, closely guarding those items that had to be kept secret: for Ben, this meant the gold ring that he had buried in the wooden handle of his old army shaving brush; the film of the surrender group at Singapore, which he had 'ponged' from the Saigon docks; and, of course, the record book.

'"You'll never go home," they used to tell us.'

The train moved off, and at last the men left Kinsayok behind them – but never their memories of what had happened there.

They headed south, past Tarsao.

From their trucks, the prisoners could see the betel nut women: older Thai women whose mouths, gums, tongues and even teeth had all turned a dark, angry-looking red colour from a lifetime of chewing betel nuts. The men had often seen them on their treks through the jungle to and from the railway.

It was difficult not to notice the betel nut women, but the guards would point them out to the prisoners anyway:

'"You'll never go home," they'd tell us. "When the war's over, you'll stay here. You'll stay here and marry these women."'

– 34 –
Tamuang

TAMUANG was a new camp, large enough to hold several thousand prisoners. It was on the railway route, but it was only now being built – after the completion of the track – as a base from which maintenance jobs along the line and other work could be carried out. It was also to be used as a transit camp.

The camp was growing all the time, and its prisoners were continuously being ordered to build new huts for the next intake of arrivals. So there were huts ready for Ben's batch, when they reached Tamuang from Kinsayok.

The huts themselves were much as they had been at the previous place: palm thatch roofs held up by bamboo poles, with communal bamboo platforms for the prisoners to sleep on. Being new, the sleeping platforms were not yet crawling with insects as the ones at Kinsayok had been; that, inevitably, would change.

Ben had not been at Tamuang long when, perched on his bed slats, he suddenly felt uncontrollably cold and his teeth started to chatter as if his jaw had gone into some kind of a frenzy.

He knew what the cause was, having seen it happen to so many others; the other prisoners in the hut, many of whom had by now had the same experience themselves, knew what was happening to him too. More importantly, they knew what needed to be done.

Ben lay down and pulled his rice sack over him. Immediately another of the prisoners placed his own rice sack on top of Ben's for further warmth, and then another added his, and then another. Soon he was lying there, shivering under the weight of fifteen rice sacks.

It was malaria and the only surprise was that he had not fallen victim to it sooner. With so much of their skin exposed and no mosquito nets, the prisoners had been bitten by insects persistently over a long period – not only on their bug-infested bed slats, but throughout the long days spent in the pest-ridden jungle.

Malaria, sooner or later, was almost inevitable.

'The treatment for it was quinine and, as almost all the world's quinine came from Java and Sumatra, the Japanese had effectively taken total possession of it. Yet they only gave us a quarter of what our medical people knew – and told them – was the correct dosage.'

The guards, by contrast, were taking quinine every day.

'We took the small amount that we were given, but it was in powder form. Quinine was horribly bitter on its own, which is why it was normally taken as a sugar-coated pill; the powder, even with a drink, was just too bitter to keep down.

So we'd get a bit of paper from somewhere – anywhere – and then put the quinine in it, screw up the paper and swallow the paper with as much water as we could get to drown it down.

But even then, a quarter of the correct dosage obviously wasn't enough. It was never cured.'

After two to three hours of shivering, Ben was onto the next stage: heat. The symptoms went into reverse, and he began to feel hotter and hotter until he was sweating profusely all over. Eventually all fifteen rice sacks were soaking wet, which meant that the worst – for now – was over. A prisoner took away the lowest – and wettest – rice sack and left it outside in the sun to dry; then another prisoner took the next rice sack, and so on.

It followed a set pattern. On the day following this attack – Day 2 – he was free of these extremes of temperature, but extremely weak. On Day 3 the extremes of temperature returned, but less violently than before; on Day 4 he was free of them again, and on Day 5 – the last day of the cycle – they came back again but in a still milder form.

Two weeks on, the whole cycle repeated itself. He went through the entire cycle twenty-four times.

The consequences would have been more serious if he had gone down with malaria sooner, during the early days at Kinsayok. Prisoners with malaria had been forced to work in the *Speedo*, and many had died as a result.

Instead, Ben's work at Tamuang was much as it had been before: assisting Captain MacDonald in the camp office, but also often going out onto the railway to carry out routine jobs.

Captain MacDonald took over as camp adjutant, the same role he had performed at Kinsayok. Until his arrival, the job at Tamuang had been carried out by a captain from another regiment, who had become widely disliked by the prisoners:

'He wasn't very popular. I'd only just arrived in Tamuang, so I didn't really know why.

My main recollection is of him having broken his arm – I can't remember how. He fell asleep one afternoon with the arm in plaster, and woke up to find a very large inscription on it: "It's a pity it wasn't your bloody neck!"'

Colonel Hugonin and Colonel Lilly had both moved to Tamuang too, but the Japanese commandant placed another colonel – 'Knocker' Knights – in overall charge.

Hugonin, however, remained responsible for Saigon Battalion. Conscious that so many of his original group were either still in Saigon or dispersed around other camps along the railway, Hugonin asked Ben if he could borrow the record book so that his officers could draw up a duplicate which he could use. The job was divided amongst his officers who each copied out a set number of pages, after which Hugonin returned the book to Ben.

So there were now two identical manuscripts of the book, but only one of the two – the original that Ben kept in the camp office – bore the Japanese stamp of approval.

◆

One morning, Ben was on the railway with a maintenance work party when the sound of an aeroplane could be heard in the distance. The roar of the engine became louder and, as it came into view, what looked like thousands of tiny speckles of gold floated down from it, glistening in the sun. They dispersed over a wide area, including where the men were working.

'They were yellow leaflets. The guards told us just to leave them, but I picked one up – a lot of us did. They'd been dropped by American pilots and the leaflets were warnings to the local population – printed in Thai – to keep well away from the area: more Allied planes would be coming, and they were going to bomb the railway.'

Shortly after that the bombs came down, disrupting the movement of Japanese soldiers and weapons into Burma. It was a development that the prisoners had longed for, but which they had also dreaded.

At first the damage was minor, but it did mean that the track was regularly needing essential repairs. Soon, increasing numbers of prisoners were being sent out onto the railway – where they were at direct risk of being bombed – as the work to be done there became more urgent. The men were being driven harder now than in recent months, and there was some return to the days of unfit prisoners being made to work.

They were being sent out on other jobs too.

It was not as bad as before, but any qualms about world opinion regarding the treatment of Allied prisoners had passed.

– *35* –

Letters

AFTER many months – and sometimes well over a year – of hearing nothing, there would be an unexpected delivery of letters from home.

The arrival of post raised hopes and tensions around the camp. Most letters sent from home never arrived, and many prisoners queued and scrambled only to find that there was nothing for them; others, whose families wrote to them practically every day, received only one or two of the letters that had been sent.

News received was not always good – the death of a parent or a brother killed in action – but there were other surprises too:

'We had two men in my hut from the same regiment – I'll call them Tim and Billy. They'd grown up together and been friends since childhood. Their wives were very good friends too.

We were in our hut, reading our letters. Tim didn't have any, but Billy did have one. It was from Billy's wife, and it contained a passage that said something like this:

"We were all so upset to learn the awful news about Tim from the War Office. Kay was heartbroken."'

The letter went on to say that Kay – Tim's 'widow' – had remarried.

'But Tim wasn't dead at all. He was standing right next to Billy, and was reading the letter over his shoulder.

Tim just burst into tears.'

When the next delivery came, there was post for Ben. The prisoners took their letters back to their huts to read them there.

'Anything interesting?' asked the prisoner sitting next to Ben when he could see that he had finished reading. Ben told him what it had said.

The prisoner sprang to his feet, jumped up onto the bed slats and called for silence. He had an announcement to make: Ben's brother Harry, captured by the Germans, had escaped!

Nobody at Tamuang, except for Ben, had ever met Harry. That did not matter: the hut reverberated with the sound of cheering.

♦

Even good news from home could be unsettling. Just a simple letter stirred thoughts of family and reminded prisoners of the hopelessness of their predicament, with no idea of when – or whether – they would ever go back to their own lives.

That is why so many of them were pleased to learn that they had been selected to leave for Japan. It was not freedom, but it was a way out of their present surroundings and a distraction from everything that they had come to associate with the railway.

Tamuang's fittest prisoners had been chosen for this. Not all were keen to leave: some preferred to remain with what they knew, and many were reluctant to turn their backs on sick friends in Thailand. So there was some swapping of places until the group that finally left Tamuang in June 1944 – which did not include Ben – was made up of prisoners who were generally willing to go.

They had no real idea of why they were needed for Japan. They simply felt that it could only be an improvement on where they were now.

Many of the Japan party were from Saigon Battalion. Perhaps they should have known better than to have such high hopes: the fittest men were wanted for Japan, just as the fittest had been selected for the railway twelve months earlier.

36

News

ONE EVENING IN JUNE 1944, the Japanese commandant made a rare appearance at *Tenko*. He said he had an announcement to make that might be of interest to the prisoners: British and American troops, he told them, had landed in vast numbers in northern France.

It was the best news that the men had heard since the start of the war, and they were astonished that the commandant had gone out of his way to tell them.

In stark contrast to this, news of events in the Far East was ruthlessly suppressed. The Japanese knew that starving the prisoners of information left them powerless; the prisoners understood this too. Perpetually kept in the dark, the men felt vulnerable and isolated. They were always anxious to know more than they did.

There was an absolute ban on radios. This was nothing new: the ban had been in place since the early days at Saigon. But, over time, the searches of prisoners' huts had escalated and intensified. These raids had long ceased to be announced in advance, and were increasingly being sprung upon the prisoners at night.

The Japanese had repeatedly warned that being caught with a radio would carry the most unthinkable consequences. It was well known among the men – from what they had heard from fellow prisoners who had been at other camps – that this was no idle threat: anybody found to have a radio might as well have been caught trying to escape.

All the prisoners understood this, but they were so desperate for information that there were still some hidden radios at Tamuang. The radios were well concealed, some of them being discreetly built into the insides of army water bottles. The batteries were smuggled in through the efforts and bravery of a sympathetic Thai trader known as Boon Pong.

The officers had a radio in their hut too, hidden beneath their bed slats. It was secretly used as a source of news to provide to the other prisoners – but very sparingly. They kept it buried under the ground and normally left it there for days at a time, in order to minimise the risk of being found out.

It was only ever dug up in the middle of the night, with several officers standing outside to keep a lookout. Inside the hut, the radio would be tuned in to the BBC in Delhi. Usually just two men listened to it, with the volume kept down very low. Once they had heard enough, they switched it off and buried it again as fast as they could.

The next day, they would sift through what they had heard to decide how much of it could safely be mentioned to the other prisoners. Great care was taken, and the news was always at least a few days old by the time any of it was passed on. This delay ensured that the prisoners only received the kind of information which could have filtered through to the camp from outside by word of mouth. The very latest news – which could only have been picked up by radio – was kept back.

The guards also withheld news from other sources, but not with anything like the intensity surrounding radios.

In some respects, they were surprisingly lax. There were prisoners, for instance, who had the job of cleaning and tidying the Japanese camp office, and it was remarkably easy for them to take oddments and items of stationery while they were in there. They normally passed these to the prisoners' camp office, which was how Captain MacDonald had obtained the notepad for Ben's record book.

They would also take news cuttings and bulletins that they found on the desks in the Japanese office, and show them to Philip Cox – a prisoner who had a reasonable grasp of written Japanese. Unfortunately the bulletins rarely said anything of much interest, which was probably why they had been left lying around in the first place.

On one occasion, however, Philip Cox came into the Allies' camp office to show Ben a news item taken from the Japanese quarters which he felt Ben needed to see.

It concerned over two thousand Australian and British prisoners, crammed into two tiny ships – 'hellships' – destined for Japan. A week after setting sail from Singapore, both ships had been torpedoed by American submarines, whose crew could not have known that they were carrying Allied prisoners. More than a thousand were believed to have drowned.

The smaller of the two ships, the *Kachidoki Maru*, had been carrying most of the men who had left the camp for Japan several weeks earlier, hoping for a better life. The administration office had a list of them: there were over a hundred from Saigon Battalion.

Three years had passed since Ben had left home. Even after all this time and all this death, a calamity on this scale was unimaginable.

Later, he took out the record book. It was dangerous to include too much detail: the prisoners were not supposed to have received this news and the Allies' office was more vulnerable to searches now than it had ever been before. Nor was it safe to place too much faith in the record book's stamp of approval: much of the information in the book was considerably more recent than the date of the stamp.

So he opened the book, went through the list, and pencilled a cryptic letter 'M' (for *Maru*, the word that ended the name of every Japanese ship) against the names of each of the shipwrecked men.

37

Rosh Hashanah

A CAPTAIN from another regiment approached Ben. All Ben knew about him was that he played a key role in the operation of the radio in the officers' hut and in the dissemination of news to the prisoners.[16]

'What are we going to do for *Rosh Hashanah*?' he asked Ben.

Ben was surprised: it had never crossed his mind that the captain was Jewish. Clearly he was, however, as he was talking about the Jewish New Year.

There had not been a *Rosh Hashanah* service since leaving home; this year, they agreed, might be different.

The number of prisoners at Tamuang varied considerably from one day to the next: large numbers would arrive at the camp en route to somewhere else, stay for a short time, and then move on. Tamuang currently had a population of about four thousand, suggesting that there should be enough Jewish prisoners among them to justify holding a short service.

After obtaining the necessary permissions a notice was displayed, stating that a Jewish New Year service would be held on the camp and naming Ben as the point of contact.

Another prisoner, on seeing the announcement, sought Ben out – this time, somebody Ben already knew:

---

[16] Later on – after he had been moved to another camp – the captain was betrayed to the Japanese military police, who interrogated him about his radio activities; he was then sent to the infamous Outram Road Jail in Singapore. Fortunately for him, the war ended a month later.

*'It was Paul Grant, from back home. I knew him very well.
I'd no idea that he'd got caught up in the Far East.*

*We had no prayer books, and so I told him that we'd agreed
on a short selection of hymns and songs that most of us should
be able to remember.*

*Then, to my astonishment, he asked what we were going to
have to eat and drink to celebrate. I knew him well enough to be
able to see from his face that he wasn't joking.'*

Ben wondered whether his old friend had gone mad.

Paul, seeing Ben's bewilderment, put his hand in his pocket –
he had shorts, rather than a loincloth – and produced a wad of
money:

*'He explained to me that he'd been driving Japanese army
trucks for them – that was one of the jobs he'd been given on his
previous camp. He'd seen that the Japanese soldiers on the
trucks with him would flog whatever they could to the local Thai
people for money. They'd sell them petrol, tyres, spanners,
wheels – anything they could get onto the truck and offload.'*

So Paul Grant had decided to do the same. He had secretly
been taking items off the trucks, and selling them to the locals.

He did not normally carry a large sum of money in his
pocket; he passed it to the Allies' office on his camp, where it
would be used or put aside for the good of the prisoners. But at
this particular time – just being in Tamuang for a few days en
route from one camp to the next – he had the money on him.

*'He knew how dangerous it was: dealing with the locals was
strictly prohibited. If he'd been spotted stealing – or just been
found with all that money – he'd have been handed straight over
to the Kempeitai. He'd probably have been for the chop.'*

The Kempeitai were the Japanese military police, always
lurking in the background like a dark, sinister presence.

Paul and Ben went to the cookhouse and explained the position. The cookhouse staff used the money to purchase some eggs from the camp shop, which they mixed into rice to make what were, in effect, rice cakes. They supplemented these with a coffee substitute, by roasting some rice over an open flame until it was dark brown and then grinding it into tiny particles.

The service was held in a corner of the camp square. Some forty prisoners attended – a direct result of the camp being so full at that time. Over the next two days, most of these men left for other camps.

By *Yom Kippur*, the Day of Atonement, the camp was down to only five Jewish prisoners. A service was held for that too, but it was marred by the presence of the assistant Japanese interpreter who hung around the men throughout the service looking vaguely bemused.

◆

The little available news suggested that the Japanese were, perhaps, no longer in the ascendency. The increasing numbers of wounded Japanese seen coming back down the railway from Burma seemed to support that view:

'But there were guards who'd do their best to convince us to the contrary. There was one who'd come up to a few of us and rattle off a list of islands that he said the Japanese had taken in the past week. It was a pretty long list – probably the same list each time he did it.

Eventually he'd dry up, so we'd try to help him out. "What about Wales?" one of us would say. He'd look a bit blank for a moment, but then realise he had to keep going. "Yes, Wales too. We took Wales." "Isle of Wight?" we'd ask. "Yes, we took Isle of Wight. Fierce fighting, but Japanese soldiers very good. We took Isle of Wight. Very strong fighters, very strong fighters."'

– 38 –
The Kempeitai

SOON after the fall of Singapore, Tom Cobham's mother had received a letter from the War Office notifying her that her son had been killed in action.

Nearly two years later, she received a standard form postcard bearing Tom's signature. She took it to the War Office, who checked their records and confirmed that, sadly, the original notification was correct: Tom was dead.

She went back to the War Office after she received a second postcard from him, and then again when she received a third. She was given the same answer each time.

If the story that Tom Cobham told Ben many years later is to be believed, he and his mother visited the War Office together after he had come home. Tom's presence in the room cut no ice with the officials: the records showed beyond question that Tom Cobham had died at Singapore.

The reason I introduce Tom Cobham here is that he and another prisoner, Adam Stock, had spent much of their lives in the Far East and were both reasonably fluent in Thai. They were among a large number at Tamuang, many of them friends of Ben, who had fought with the Malayan Volunteer Forces before the surrender at Singapore.

Since first arriving at Tamuang, Cobham and Stock had regularly crept out of the camp at night and made friends with sympathetic members of the local Thai population. They would return from these excursions with news and, more particularly, money.

Cobham and Stock were accompanied on these outings by the legendary Colonel 'Knocker' Knights – a small but very forceful man with a passing resemblance to Mr Punch. Knights had moved to Tamuang from Tarsao some months earlier and been placed in charge of all the camp's prisoners – British, Australian and Dutch – by the Japanese commandant.

'Colonel Knights was a very highly decorated First World War veteran.

He must have been about twenty years older than most of us. So to be going out on dangerous night-time escapades was exceptionally courageous at his age – and particularly so given his prominent position on the camp.

His absence was far more likely to be noticed than most other people's, and if he was caught his punishment no doubt would be especially brutal just to make an example out of him.'

It was extremely dangerous for Cobham and Stock too.

There were monetary rewards for handing over prisoners who broke out of the camp and – with no occupying Western power – white faces stood out even more here than in Saigon.

If any of them were caught, they would find themselves facing every prisoner's worst nightmare: the Kempeitai.

♦

It had been the dreaded Kempeitai – the secret police arm of the Imperial Japanese Army – who had tortured and executed Tucker and Wade after their failed escape attempt, during the early days at Saigon.

The very mention of the Kempeitai sent shivers down prisoners' spines – and most of the guards' spines too. Trained in torture and wholly without mercy, they unhesitatingly inflicted the most unspeakable torment on those that they arrested – whether to extract information from them or simply to punish or deter. Nothing was considered to be too bestial or too cruel. And torture, usually, was followed by execution.

The Kempeitai had been in the background since the start, but now their role was becoming more prominent.

They started to appear at the camp unannounced; all the guards, regardless of rank, jumped to attention and were tense and uneasy in their presence. The Kempeitai's role included the running of the prisoner-of-war and labour camps, and so the guards – treated with contempt by the Kempeitai – were all directly answerable to them.

When the Kempeitai came to the camp, they would conduct searches of the prisoners' huts. These searches seemed to make the guards almost as nervous as they made the prisoners: the guards were fearful that the Kempeitai would find something that they themselves had missed – which was why the guards' own searches had become so much more aggressive and more frequent.

It was during one of these searches that the Kempeitai found some forbidden radios:

'It started with two brothers, who were taken away to the local Kempeitai headquarters for questioning. They were beaten up viciously in the course of their interrogation – as was practically everyone who came into the Kempeitai's hands.

All the obvious questions: how they'd got the radio, who ran it, where they'd got the batteries and so on. It was like throwing stones into a pond – the ripples went further and further, and the Kempeitai gradually roped in more and more POWs.

There were a lot taken in from Tamuang for questioning, and I don't remember seeing any of them come back.

When a prisoner was handed over to the Kempeitai, then normally that was it. We'd never see him again.'

39

The Pit

LOOKING DOWN over the Pacific Ocean, a lone Japanese pilot saw a huge Allied warship sailing some distance away. With extraordinary speed and accuracy, he manoeuvred his tiny aircraft until it was directly above the ship and, flying backwards and forwards over the length of the vessel, dropped all his bombs on it.

Each bomb did the maximum possible damage, leaving nothing and nobody intact except for the captain and the part of the ship that he was standing on at the time.

The Japanese pilot was nothing if not thorough. As the ship's captain looked up at him from the bridge, the pilot swooped down low, leaned out of his small aircraft and – with a single stroke of his samurai sword – sliced the captain's head off.

'A guard had told us that story a year or so earlier. We hadn't been so stupid as to believe it then, and none of the guards would dream of trying to tell us anything like that now. They no longer had the swagger that they'd had before: most of them by this stage had grown tense and nervy.

We knew that the tide had turned against them – and they knew that we knew.'

The prisoners knew this partly from the carefully distributed information picked up from the radio in the officers' hut, but the real signs were everywhere to be seen.

The men increasingly saw for themselves that the railway was being used to bring more and more wounded Japanese troops out of Burma – the opposite of its intended purpose – and that relatively few men or materials were being sent in. Meanwhile, the Allies' bombing of the railway continued to intensify.

Each successful hit on the line meant more prisoners being sent out on repair work, with further consequences:

'One train was bringing prisoners, who'd been out on repairs, back to their camp. The trucks were too small to hold them all, so a lot of the men perched on the roofs while the Japanese guards who'd gone out with them stayed inside.

Then, suddenly, they were spotted by American planes. The Americans circled round, took aim and started to drop bombs directed at the trucks. The train stopped and its driver and everyone else – guards and POWs – sprang away and scampered off into the surrounding jungle.

The pilots had noticed them and assumed they were all Japanese, so the planes just fired into the jungle where they'd seen them disappear. They flew round and round in circles overhead, killing POWs as well as guards.'

There were other American bombers in the sky too – not just over the railway. They usually came over at night; viewed from the camp, their target seemed to lie somewhere in the direction of Bangkok.

So what did it all mean for the prisoners?

Ever since their capture, they had repeatedly been told that surrender was unthinkable to the Japanese: better to die than to return home defeated. The Japanese would fight to the last.

The guards seemed to have lost their swashbuckling poise of a year ago, but their demeanour was just as aggressive. The endless, frantic searching for radios and the increasing involvement of the Kempeitai indicated a changed mood: a more suspicious view of the prisoners than before, with a different, edgier kind of hostility towards them.

How much edgier still would they become if the Allies were ever to land in Thailand? With a ground war on their hands (as well as a food shortage), would the Japanese Imperial Army carry on diverting manpower – and rice – to the guarding and feeding of thousands of Allied prisoners?

These were not new worries: they had preyed on prisoners' minds since the start. The Japanese had certainly not seemed interested in taking or keeping prisoners during the jungle fighting in Malaya.

◆

Then came a new development: the pit.

The men were ordered to build a tall fence along one outside edge of the camp; along the camp's other three surrounding edges – more ominously – they were to dig an enormous ditch: ten feet deep and ten feet across.

They piled up the excavated earth along the outside rim of the huge ditch. This created a sloping wall of soil – reaching at least fifteen feet up from the bottom of the pit – around the perimeter of the camp. In one place, there was to be a bridge to enable the prisoners to go to and from work, usually for railway repairs. The bridge would be closely guarded at all times.

When the pit was finished, a gigantic machine gun was built into each of the four corners of the large rectangular boundary that now surrounded the prisoners. The four massive guns pointed inwards – at the camp.

The men were told that this was to prevent anyone escaping, but that made no sense: escape had been practically impossible from the start. A more believable purpose was to deter any attempt at a mass breakout, should the Allies land in Thailand.

But even that seemed unlikely. If the Japanese were concerned that the Allies would launch a land invasion, and that the prisoners – already a burden – would pose a potential threat, then they had a far more obvious motive for surrounding the camp with machine guns and a vast, yawning pit.

40

Divide and Rule

THOSE PRISONERS WHO HAD SURVIVED THE SINKING of the *Kachidoki Maru* – the ship bound for Japan – had all jumped within the first ten minutes.

More than half of the Saigon Battalion men on board either drowned in the South China Sea or were eaten by sharks. The rest were later picked up by Japanese trawlers and continued their voyage to Japan.

There they were put to work in coal mines and zinc foundries, under truly abominable working conditions. Hopes of a better life had come to nothing.

But other survivors, who had sailed on the accompanying ship, were instead rescued by American submarines and brought back to safety.

On arriving home, they provided the authorities with the first first-hand accounts of what had happened on the railway.

♦

In the closing weeks of 1944, the Secretary of State for War conveyed this new information to the House of Commons.

The details were more specific, and even grimmer, than the Foreign Secretary's statement had been at the start of the year. He spoke of the railway's 'appalling death rate, the lowest estimate of deaths being one in five'.

The tens of thousands of waiting families were at least spared the knowledge that their loved ones in Thailand – if still alive – were now digging fortified trenches around their camps.

The Japanese did not react to the statement (as they had to the previous one) by displaying any particular qualms about world opinion. Instead the relentless searches continued and the prisoners remained surrounded by the huge pits and machine guns. Meanwhile, outside the camps, the Kempeitai continued to torture and kill.

Then a further development was announced: all officers, with the exception of the doctors, were to be transferred to separate camps.

The thinking behind this move was clearly that the prisoners would be less able to act without the organisation and leadership of their officers. But it raised the same question that the pit and the four machine guns had: Why now, suddenly? Why now, after all this time?

What action did the Japanese fear that the prisoners might take, for which they would need the leadership of their officers? An attempted breakout from the camp, perhaps, if the Allies should land in Thailand?

Or an armed revolt, should the guards turn the machine guns on them? The prisoners were unarmed, but the guards could not be certain of that: increasingly the guards and the Kempeitai were searching not only for radios, but for guns.

In January 1945, the officers left for their new camp in Kanburi.

With the mounting intensity of the checks and searches, Colonel Hugonin needed to find a way of smuggling his copy of Ben's record book into his new camp:

'The officers undid the binding of the colonel's copy, split the book up into separate sheets and distributed the loose pages between them.

The army haversacks had a double layer of webbing at the base end for added strength. Several officers unstitched their double-webbing, slipped the sheets in between the two layers, and then stitched it all back up.'

That was how Hugonin's copy of the book was carried to Kanburi: with the pages distributed among a number of different officers and embedded into the fabric of their haversacks.

♦

With the officers (except for the doctors) gone from the camp, some organisational changes had to be made at Tamuang.

The Japanese would not allow the medical officers to have any formal role in the running of the camp: they were there only to treat the sick. After them, the next highest-ranking prisoner was a regimental sergeant-major, RSM Christopher. With Colonel 'Knocker' Knights now at the officers' camp, RSM Christopher assumed overall responsibility for the prisoners at Tamuang.

Captain MacDonald had gone to Kanburi with the other officers, and so somebody was needed to run the camp's administration office. RSM Christopher chose Ben for this role.

Ben was now effectively the camp adjutant (but still only a lance-bombardier, and so outranked by many of the other prisoners). This placed him in charge of general administration, but his new position was going to involve something far more awkward than that:

'It fell to me to look after the secret cash box. I already knew about it: it was a wooden box, it was reasonably full, and it contained money that we weren't supposed to have.

It was quite large too – probably about ...'

He pictured the cash box in his mind and, with his hands, indicated its dimensions: long enough and wide enough to hold a substantial amount of money, with enough space to keep notes and coins of different values segregated from each other.

Visualising the large cash box in this way seemed to bring an uncomfortable, almost haunted look to his face.

I was soon to find out why.

41

The Cash Box

SENTRIES patrolled the outside of the pit, twenty-four hours a day.

In spite of that, Tom Cobham and Adam Stock continued to disappear from the camp at night unnoticed. Unlike before, however, they were no longer accompanied by 'Knocker' Knights (who had been moved to the officers' camp), and they now had the additional obstacle of having to cross the pit:

'It was very wide and very deep, but they still managed to get across it using a bamboo pole.

The pole was furtively placed across the pit after dark, and used as a rather precarious bridge.'

Once they were out of the camp, they did much the same as they had been doing all along: visiting their Thai contacts, picking up news and collecting whatever money their friends had been able to raise for them.

Then they climbed back along the bamboo pole, across the treacherous pit, to be back at the camp before daybreak.

Whichever one of them had the money would pass it to Ben for the cash box – and that was where matters became complicated.

The Japanese did not pay each prisoner individually; instead an aggregate amount was calculated to cover the number of prisoners and days worked, and then that total sum of money was provided in cash to Ben in the camp administration office.

Ben deducted a proportion of this sum for the doctors and medical orderlies, so that they could buy food for the men in the sick huts. He distributed the rest among the individual prisoners, according to the number of days worked by each of them.

But normally the sick huts still needed more money, even after they had received their percentage of the total payroll; the sick prisoners were in greater need of food from the camp shop than the others.

So Ben also gave the medical officers some of the money that Cobham and Stock brought into the camp. That money would then be spent in the shop.

The rest of what Cobham and Stock brought back was kept in the cash box.

'That meant more money was being spent in the camp shop than the Japanese had issued to our men in pay. The Japanese weren't slow to spot that, and from time to time RSM Christopher and I would be summoned into the Japanese camp office and asked why.

Our stock answer – the same one that had been used since the early days in Saigon – was that our men had been selling their belongings to some of the Japanese guards. Somehow we got away with that reply, even though we'd all been ordered to hand in our valuables a long time ago.

Selling to the Japanese, incidentally, wasn't prohibited. What wasn't allowed was for us to have any kinds of dealings with the local population – which was what Cobham and Stock were doing.'

Then there were the different denominations:

'The money the Japanese gave us to pay the men came in a variety of denominations; so did the money that Tom Cobham and Adam Stock came back with. But, generally, the denominations of the notes that Cobham and Stock brought back tended to be higher.'

That was not surprising: any individual prisoner's pay was very low, and so the Japanese issued the money in small denominations. The same considerations did not apply to the sums raised by Cobham and Stock.

'I had to be extremely careful that the extra money spent in the camp shop wasn't in higher denominations than the POWs' pay.

So long as we made sure of that, we could stick to our story that the extra money was the result of prisoners selling their belongings to the Japanese guards.

But if the denominations spent in the shop were too high, they'd know that story wasn't true – because the guards were probably being paid in low denominations also.'

In other words:

'We had to make sure that the right kinds of notes were being kept in the cash box, and the right kinds of notes were being distributed.

So one of the first things I did was to put Don Chadwick – another of the Volunteer Malayan Forces, like Tom Cobham and Adam Stock – in charge of running the camp shop.

Don was also a chartered accountant, and so we both spoke the same language. Between us, we made absolutely certain that, whatever the takings were from the camp shop, the money was swapped for the right denominations before we handed it over to the Japanese office: we just couldn't afford to slip up.

If we got caught out – if they twigged that there was money being spent in the shop that could only have come in from outside the camp – then we knew that they'd call in the Kempeitai.

And then all hell would break loose.'

♦

Ben kept the cash box buried under the ground, directly beneath his bed slats.

When he received money for the cash box, he did not routinely dig the box up but found somewhere else to hide it for the time being – usually in a well-concealed gap in the hut's bamboo structure.

But that had its dangers too, and so every week or so the cash box had to be unearthed, so that new money could be put into it or so that sums needed for a specific purpose could be taken out:

'We only ever dug it up in the middle of the night, and always under strict surveillance with POWs guarding the entrances to the hut inside and outside to keep a lookout.

Once we'd dug it up, I'd put the money in or swap it for different denominations, and then we'd bury it again under my bed slats. We had to be extremely vigilant and very, very fast.'

Then there were the searches – sometimes the guards, and sometimes the Kempeitai. There was never any warning:

'They'd just descend on us, and the frequency and ruthlessness of these visits just got worse and worse.

Previously we'd stood to attention by our bed slats while they went through our kits and searched around, but not any more. The moment they turned up they'd just push everyone out of the hut, and we'd stand outside while they went through our belongings and hunted about furiously.

We'd see them go in with spades. All we could do was just wait outside, knowing that they were digging the place up.

I'd die a million deaths standing out there – not being able to see where they were digging and just hoping against hope that they wouldn't find the cash box.'

After what felt like an endless wait, the prisoners would see them coming out of the hut with their spades.

The search was over – until next time.

Leaving the Railway

THE BRIDGE ON THE RIVER KWAI, as it later became known, was the largest bridge on the railway. It was easily visible from Tamuang, and the men saw several bombing raids over it in the first half of 1945.

The sight of American aircraft circling over the bridge stirred mixed emotions: fear for the safety of prisoners on the ground, but excitement at the prospect of an imminent assault on one of the railway's most prominent landmarks.

Yet the damage was normally fixable: it only led to further repairs, with cargo having to be transported across the river by barge in the meantime. It was not until June that Ben saw the decisive raid which finally put the bridge out of action.

There had been a positive development the previous month: word on the camp that Germany had surrendered. The sources and the prevalence of the rumours pointed to their being true.

Unlike D-Day a year earlier, the men had not heard about this from the Japanese. That was not surprising: hostility and suspicion towards the prisoners – the pits, the machine guns, the fanatical searches – had soared since then.

It was time, again, to move on.

Almost all of those still at Tamuang were to transfer to another camp – this time, well away from the railway that they had built.

The prisoners took stock of their belongings and considered whether there were items that it might be safer to leave behind.

For Ben, there were four items in particular: the gold ring his father had given him; the film of the Singapore surrender that he had 'ponged' from the Saigon docks; his record book of the thousand men; and – hardest of all to hide – the cash box.

The gold ring was no problem. For over three years, it had been embedded in the wooden handle of his shaving brush and had never aroused any suspicion. He would bring that with him.

The record book was more dangerous. The camp office – like everywhere else – was frequently being searched and, although the book had escaped so far, it had become clear that its stamp of approval was of limited protection. But he could not abandon it now: the book was almost certainly more up-to-date than Colonel Hugonin's copy of it, and it could not be assumed anyway that Hugonin's copy would survive the war.

The surrender film was a harder decision. He had successfully concealed it for nearly three years – for most of that time in the thatched roofs of the huts he had slept in since coming to Thailand. He did not want to relinquish it now, but the risks were growing and he had to face facts. Reluctantly, he took the film to the camp latrines and dropped it in.

The cash box raised a different kind of question: not whether to bring it, but how. The only option was to load it onto the trucks with the other variously sized crates and boxes, and hope that it would not attract any interest.

Ben was in the last of three groups, each of five hundred men, to leave Tamuang for their new destination.

They headed along the railway towards Bangkok; with the risk of air attack, rail movement was restricted to the hours of darkness. It was then that they saw the true extent of the Allied bombing for themselves: rail communications were in chaos and several of the main bridges along the route had been destroyed. The journey of under two hundred miles was so delayed and disrupted by the river crossings that it took five days to reach their destination, about a hundred miles from Bangkok.

It was a place called Pratchai.

– 43 –
Pratchai

SHORTLY AFTER REACHING PRATCHAI, two-thirds of the prisoners – including many light sick – were moved to another camp to build an airstrip. Conditions there proved to be intolerable, but that is a separate story: Ben was among the six hundred who remained at Pratchai.

The camp at Pratchai was mostly built by the time that Ben's group arrived there. The huts were constructed in the same way as on the previous camps, and the overall layout was similar too.

The main job still to be completed was the one that the men had finished at Tamuang only a few months earlier: digging pits.

Now the prisoners had to start digging all over again: a deep, wide, rectangular ditch surrounding the camp, with the excavated earth piled up to form a high embankment on the outer edge. Sentries patrolled the outside of the pit day and night, and – as before – a huge machine gun was sited in each corner, pointing inwards at the camp.

The running of the camp remained as it had been at Tamuang, with RSM Christopher in charge of the prisoners and acting as their main point of contact with the Japanese commandant. As before, Christopher was the camp's highest-ranking prisoner (apart from the medical officers, whose role was still not allowed to extend to the wider running of the camp).

Ben remained in charge of administration. This included, as at Tamuang, responsibility for the cash box and everything that that demanded.

During his first night at Pratchai, Ben buried the cash box under the ground beneath his new bed slats, while others kept a lookout from each entrance to the hut in the usual way. The need for vigilance had not subsided: the huts were soon being searched again, and the ground dug up with spades.

The Allies' administration office was searched too, and Ben's record book only narrowly escaped detection.

So, the next time he and RSM Christopher were called into the Japanese office to discuss camp administration, Ben brought the record book in with him. He stood as near to the shelves alongside one of the walls as he could do without arousing suspicion and, when the moment was right, placed the book – unnoticed – among the Japanese papers on one of those shelves.

'The way I saw it was this: the place the Japanese were least likely to search for suspicious records was in their own office.'

♦

The men had been brought to Pratchai for a specific task:

'There were hills behind the camp, which made it an important area strategically.

The main job at Pratchai was to dig Japanese heavy artillery into the hillside. Their guns were being positioned to meet any oncoming Allied forces invading from Burma, and also any threat from the sea.

So another flagrant breach of the Geneva Convention. They'd threatened to annihilate us at Saigon when we'd objected to unloading guns on the docks, and since then there'd been the railway. Now this.'

For Ben, however, his life as adjutant was much the same at Pratchai as it had been before. Tom Cobham and Adam Stock still crossed the pit at night, bringing back money as they had done at Tamuang; Ben continually strove to ensure that the shop's takings were in denominations which would not give

Cobham and Stock away to the Japanese; and every few nights –
as before – Ben dug the cash box up under strict surveillance.

The spade searches continued but, in one important respect,
the circumstances had changed: the prisoners almost certainly
had no radios at Pratchai. The radios had been left at Tamuang
(they had become too dangerous) and the men were not hiding
any weapons either. So, with the guards still digging under the
huts and determined to carry on until they found something,
Ben's cash box was more vulnerable than ever before.

◆

Meanwhile, Ben's malarial attacks were starting to subside. It
had not been the most serious type:

> *'The worse kinds could lead to blackwater fever, which often
> meant kidney failure.*
>
> *Illness continued to rage and it never came to an end. More
> tropical ulcers and amputations, dysentery, and all the
> consequences of malnutrition.*
>
> *Also elephantiasis, which caused horrendous swellings,
> transmitted by mosquitoes.*
>
> *It just went on.'*

◆

Cobham and Stock normally left the camp together; they crossed
the pit at night using a bamboo pole, as they had at Tamuang.
But they often returned at different times.

They had made their way back separately on the night that
Adam Stock lost his grip on the bamboo. He fell straight down
into the pit, breaking one of his legs as he hit the bottom. Stock
lay bleeding in the mud – unable to move and trapped between
the pit walls which towered above him on each side.

When the patrolling Japanese sentry found him down there,
no concern was shown for his broken leg: the high value
banknotes that Stock had in his possession from the local Thais
were of far more interest.

Adam Stock was handed over to the local Kempeitai headquarters for questioning.

It is difficult to imagine how he could have been in worse trouble: he had broken out of the camp at night, which was seen as tantamount to attempting escape; he had been having dealings with people outside the camp, which was forbidden; he was obtaining money, which could be used to buy the prisoners influence with the locals – or even weapons; and he could collect more news by meeting Thai people and visiting them in their homes than he could ever have done with a radio hidden in his hut.

Stock knew what to expect. He was savagely beaten and interrogated under torture.

How many times, they asked him, had he crossed the ditch? Did others go with him? How much money had he built up?

Where was the money kept? Who looked after it?

Fortunately for Tom Cobham (and for Ben as the man who operated the cash box), Adam Stock did not squeal.

♦

To his astonishment, Stock was released.

If it had happened just weeks – and perhaps even days – earlier, Adam Stock would almost certainly have been executed. Luckily, the timing had been on his side.

Everything was about to change.

Something About a Bomb

THE FIRST SIGN came when three of the Japanese guards lit a bonfire on the camp square, just a few yards away from their office hut. They seemed particularly intent on what they were doing, slightly harried, and rather subdued.

Soon they were going into their office, coming back out again with piles of papers, and throwing them onto the fire.

'When I saw that, my mind went straight back to those final days at Singapore. I remembered how, as soon as we'd known that we'd lost, we'd had to burn our radar notebooks.'

The prisoners spoke about it that night, as they lay on their bed slats. They had all had much the same thought that Ben had, but they dared not expect too much: to find they had been wrong would be unbearable – yet clearly it meant something.

But why, they wondered, should the guards be burning their papers? It was a prison camp: they were unlikely to be holding sensitive strategic information.

Evidence of war crimes seemed more likely; yet the camp's most compelling proof of atrocities would not come from written documents, but from the prisoners themselves. Were there plans to deal with them too? Thoughts turned to the four machine guns and to the deep, gaping pit.

Perhaps the burning of the papers meant something else: that the Japanese were expecting an imminent ground invasion, and that there would soon be no need for a camp office – or, for that matter, a camp.

Every possible theory, it seemed, led back to the ever-present machine guns.

It was hard to sleep. As the night wore on, each prisoner lay on his bed slats with his own thoughts: wary optimism, gut-wrenching fear, world-weary resignation – or constant switching between all three.

Ben felt it as much as anyone, but there was something else also: something that he had to do.

Many weeks earlier, he had left his record book in the Japanese camp office, thinking that would be the safest place for it. It was still possible, he supposed, that it might not have been thrown on the bonfire.

He levered himself up from his bamboo platform, walked out of the hut and made his way through the night towards the Japanese office.

He crept in.

The area was only dimly lit, but he remembered the part of the office where he had placed the book. He had noticed it there when he had last gone in to speak with the Japanese administrators a few days ago.

The book was still there now, in a pile with some other papers. It seemed that the guards had been burning only specific documents – not all of them. He picked up the book and returned with it to his hut.

It was just as well that he had retrieved it: Colonel Hugonin's copy (as Ben would later learn) had been destroyed many months earlier.

◆

The next morning was like any other.

The Japanese bugle call sounded, there was rice and tea followed by *Tenko*, and then most of the stronger prisoners went out on their work parties into the hills.

The rest of the men remained in the sick huts or, as in Ben's case, carried out their jobs on the camp.

But just after midday, the work parties returned. They had never previously stopped work before evening; today they had been brought back early with no explanation.

The men were mystified, but not in the way that they had been the previous night: something had happened during the morning that they could not understand, yet which appeared to be encouraging.

The Japanese guards who had come back with them seemed quiet and dejected.

RSM Christopher was called into the Japanese commandant's office. He was joined by the camp's senior medical officer, and they remained in there for some time.

A strange atmosphere pervaded the camp, as the prisoners drifted back to their huts and wondered what was going on.

They spoke about what had happened that morning:

'On their walk out to work, they'd been thronged by local Thai people, who'd been desperately trying to tell them something.

The people had seemed happy and very excited. They'd called out to the prisoners. The men couldn't understand what they were saying, but the Thais had seemed very eager to get some kind of message across to them.

They'd also made repeated, very pronounced hand signals to try and convey their message – but the men hadn't understood that either. It was clearly supposed to mean something, but the men just didn't know what to make of these gestures.'

Ben demonstrated the gestures to me with a swift upward circular movement of his hands. As he did this, his two hands moved abruptly away from each other with his fingers springing wide open.

'They seemed to be saying there'd been an explosion of some kind. Something about a bomb.'

The tension mounted as the prisoners waited anxiously in their huts and around the camp for information.

Then at last the bugle sounded. It was a call which they recognised: they were being summoned to the camp square, as they had been at least twice a day for far too long.

But this was not the Japanese *Tenko* call that they had all become so used to hearing. It was the British 'Fall In' signal – last heard three and a half years ago at Singapore and prohibited from use ever since:

'A tremendous roar of relief broke out all over the camp – it's a wonder we didn't raise the thatched roofs off our huts.
It could only mean one thing.'

Instantly – running, limping and crawling – prisoners surged from all directions towards the parade ground. Those who had been caught on the latrines when the bugle sounded bolted straight off to the meeting area without their loincloths.

Within moments the men were gathered together in a large, excitable mass on the camp square. The British senior medical officer (who outranked RSM Christopher) stood on the raised platform that was normally used by the Japanese officer at *Tenko*. The noise dropped and the men looked at him expectantly.

Then he finally said it: 'Good news – the war's over!'

Shouts and yelps of irrepressible joy burst out across the parade ground. As if from nowhere, three Union Jacks appeared (until now kept hidden under prisoners' bed slats), and then a Dutch flag. They were tied to bamboo poles and hoisted up to the sounds of tumultuous cheers.

'We all started hugging each other and openly crying with happiness – crying unashamedly, the tears just rolling down our faces.
We'd hoped for this moment for years and dreamt that one day it might arrive. But we'd never known that it would.'

The senior medical officer had to wait for several minutes before he could continue speaking.

When he did, he announced that the Japanese guards would retain control of the camp until the arrival of relieving forces; the men in the meantime were to remain there and cause no trouble. After everything that they had survived, the worst outcome now, he said, would be to provoke an incident: the guns dug into the hillside overlooked the camp, and they could still – as he put it – 'blast the lot of us to Kingdom come'.

The men stayed on the camp square when the parade was over, supremely happy but also, now, slightly dazed: a mixture of relief and disbelief.

Slowly they began to speak with each other about what had happened, about freedom, and about what lay ahead:

'We talked about what we were going to do when we got home, who we couldn't wait to see, and how all the problems of normal life could never bother us again – not after what we'd been through.'

They did not go back to their huts that night: they just walked up and down the camp square, discussing the day's events and their hopes for the future. They continued through the dark hours and were still out on the square, talking to each other about going home, as the first signs of light appeared.

It was morning again. There would be no work parties today.

45

Order to Kill

CAPTAIN BRADLEY of the Scots Guards arrived at the camp in the early afternoon.

He was plainly not a prisoner. He was smartly uniformed, well built, and too light-skinned to have been subjected to prolonged exposure to the tropical sun. In fact he was new to the region, having been parachuted down by the RAF.

The prisoners directed him to Ben, who knew why Captain Bradley was there and found him the Japanese interpreter. The interpreter bowed to Bradley, who then asked him to fetch the camp commandant. The interpreter left and returned shortly afterwards, still on his own.

'Captain Suzuki is sleeping,' he explained.[17]

'Then wake him up,' barked Bradley. 'I want to see him straight away. Go and fetch Captain Suzuki and all the other guards – Japanese and Korean – and bring them all here. Now.'

Just minutes later, the guards were all assembled. Following some long-drawn-out bowing formalities, Bradley produced a camera and photographed each one of them, noting their names and numbers. The war crimes process had begun.

---

[17] Earlier in the war, a Captain Suzuki – perhaps even the same one – had been the commandant at one of the railway camps. While he was there, several large mailbags of letters were delivered for the prisoners – the first to arrive for them since they had been captured. This coincided, however, with a failed escape attempt by seven men who had been caught and brought back. As a collective punishment, Suzuki assembled all the prisoners on the camp square, announced that they had received their first delivery of post from home, and then made them watch as two of the guards set fire to the mailbags.

Afterwards, Captain Bradley spoke with the prisoners and told them why the Japanese, after years of proclaiming that they would fight on forever and that nothing could be more shameful than to accept defeat, had suddenly surrendered.

In the past ten days, the first two atomic bombs ever to be used – 'Little Boy' and 'Fat Man' – had been dropped on Japan. The unimaginable scale and ferocity of the resulting death and devastation had shocked the world. The nature of warfare had changed forever: so much so that Emperor Hirohito had intervened personally in his cabinet's deliberations, to order the unconditional surrender of Japan.

But the prisoners would not learn until some time later just how narrowly the bombs had saved them from total annihilation ...

♦

One year earlier, in August 1944, a written order had been sent from the Japanese War Ministry to the commandant of every prisoner-of-war camp.

The 'order to kill' (as it later became known) instructed the commandants to prepare for the final disposal of all their prisoners:

> Whether they are destroyed individually or in groups, or however it is done – with mass bombing, poisonous smoke, poisons, drowning, decapitation or whatever – dispose of them as the situation dictates.

> In any case, it is the aim not to allow the escape of a single one, to annihilate them all, and not to leave any traces.

So, in late 1944, the prisoners in Thailand had been made to dig mass graves all around their camps, which were then surrounded by heavy machine guns. The excavated earth that was piled up on the outer edges of the pits would make it easy 'not to leave any traces'.

While the Thailand prisoners were digging their trenches, far worse was happening on a distant island in the Philippines. The island was Palawan, and the events that took place there on 14 December 1944 were horrifying.

The island's prisoners were herded into air raid shelters, where they were doused in petrol and set on fire. Some, who tried to get away, were machine-gunned to death; others frantically sought to climb to safety over a cliff, only to be hunted down and bayoneted – many of them begging for mercy.

The massacre had been prompted by Japanese intelligence that Allied forces were about to land on the island. The terms of the 'order to kill' required that prisoners be obliterated on the strength of any such information, for fear that the Allied invaders might rescue them from captivity to become fighting forces again.

♦

By August 1945, the lives of over a hundred thousand Allied prisoners were hanging by a thread. Prison camp commandants throughout the Japanese-occupied territories were on standby for Allied landings, and had their execution plans in place.

The Japanese were expecting Allied ground forces to reach Thailand on or about 21 August, and were set to exterminate the prisoners there on that date. Yet the prisoners' demise may well have been even more imminent than that: the Allies had planned to invade Thailand on 18 August.

But on 6 August and 9 August, punctuated by warnings of 'prompt and utter destruction' and 'a rain of ruin from the air the like of which has never been seen on this earth', the two atomic bombs were dropped on the Japanese cities of Hiroshima and Nagasaki.

On 15 August 1945, Japan unconditionally surrendered.

The Allied invasion of Thailand – the cue to annihilate all the prisoners there – had been scheduled for three days later.

No invasion would now be necessary.

46

Bushido

A LARGE HUT stood behind the Japanese camp office, towards the area where the guards slept. RSM Christopher, accompanied by Ben and two others, asked one of the guards to show them what was in there.

The guard conferred briefly with one of his officers and then took them over to the hut. He opened the door:

'We couldn't believe our eyes. It was an Aladdin's cave of parcels and goods provided by the International Red Cross: medical supplies, tinned food, clothing – huge stacks of them.

In all this time, we'd been provided with next to nothing.'

RSM Christopher asked why none of it had been distributed.

The answer he was given was that to do so would have resulted in the prisoners being better fed than the Japanese. But that explanation could only make sense if the prisoners had already been eating as well as the guards were:

'It had been us, not them, who'd had to live off the sweepings from the warehouse floor. They'd had their own supplies of duck eggs – we hadn't; we'd been at the mercy of deliveries to the camp shop for any extras, and even then our pay had never stretched far enough. And whenever meat had become available it had gone almost entirely to them.

We still had men dying from malnutrition – the war was over, but our problems weren't. We'd desperately needed that Red Cross food, and they'd just held onto it.

It was the same with the medical supplies. Our doctors had pleaded for medicines from the start, and just been ignored – and then been beaten up when the men became too sick to work. Now we learned that the Japanese had had the medicines all this time and held them back from us while men died.

The clothing too. They'd had their uniforms, but we'd had to go through the jungle practically naked.'

The more likely explanation was the spirit of *Bushido*: the Japanese 'way of the warrior' which decreed that a soldier must fall on his sword rather than accept defeat, and that one who surrendered was worthy only of contempt:

'They'd spent three and a half years telling us that we were a disgrace, and that we should have killed ourselves rather than surrender at Singapore. Having become prisoners, whatever they did to us was better than we deserved. We should just be thankful that they'd spared our lives.

Well, now they'd surrendered. Did they all start killing themselves? Certainly none in our camp.

Instead, we suddenly had guards coming into our huts being all friendly towards us, and asking if we'd sign letters that they could show to the Allies confirming that we'd been well treated. None of us signed them, of course.

But the worst of the guards didn't bother with that. They just vanished.'

The Japanese high command had issued a formal order authorising guards who had mistreated prisoners to flee without trace; the same document had ordered the destruction of incriminating papers.

Two of the guards who fled from Pratchai – particularly vicious ones by all accounts – ran into some prisoners in Bangkok, who recognised them from another camp during their days on the railway. The prisoners cut their noses off.

47

The Forgotten Army

THE CASH BOX was worthless. The high value banknotes, obtained at such risk, had been withdrawn as legal tender.

This presented an immediate problem: the rations had not improved, and with so many sick still dangerously malnourished the camp needed to buy food from outside. So Ben and three others took a truck into the nearby town of Saburi where they stocked up with meat and vegetables:

'Luckily the shopkeepers agreed to accept IOU notes, which I wrote out and signed 'for and on behalf of His Britannic Majesty King George VI'.

I put my name and army number on them and never heard anything further. I've no doubt that they were paid.'

Back at the camp, Ben's first priority was the distribution of the Red Cross supplies – but there was another job too.

Soon after the surrender, a message was relayed to Ben from Colonel Hugonin, who was at the officers' camp at Kanburi. It was about the record book:

'You'll remember that, when the officers were leaving Tamuang, they'd unbound their copy of the book, and then divided up the pages between them and sewn them into the fabric of their haversacks.

I now learned that, on their arrival at Kanburi, the guards there had torn all the haversacks open and destroyed the pages. So a replacement copy was needed.'

The job of writing out a fresh copy from the original was shared out among a group of the camp's prisoners, while Ben dealt with the Red Cross distributions.

Before long the men on the camp were properly clothed, and the new copy of the record book – the regiment's copy, to be kept with official records on returning home – had been delivered in person to Colonel Hugonin at Kanburi.

♦

The roar of an engine could be heard over the camp. Men ran out of their huts to see what was happening.

Circling overhead was an Allied aircraft. The pilot, realising that he had spotted a prisoner-of-war camp, came down as low as he safely could and threw down his half-used packet of cigarettes onto the camp square. There was a mad scramble for them, as the pilot waved and flew off.

The next day, several larger aeroplanes appeared overhead. They had come to drop relief supplies:

'There were medicines and other fragile items, which were lowered by parachute. The rest were just dropped and fell. They were packed in thick corrugated cardboard canisters – very large and very heavy.

When we saw the planes, we all knew we had to get into our huts and keep away from the open camp square where these huge parcels were going to fall.'

But, Pratchai being a comparatively small camp, one package missed the square and fell directly onto one of the bamboo huts that the prisoners had gone into for safety. The hut was destroyed, with serious casualties for those inside and some prisoners killed.

'They'd survived Singapore and the railway and everything else. The war was over at long last – then this.

Killed by relief supplies.'

As well as food and clothing, there was news. The packages contained hundreds of copies of the *News of the World*:

> *'The newspapers were full of names and references to people and events that meant nothing to us. We'd been out of touch for so long and so much had happened in that time.*
>
> *But I remember one aspect more than anything else: there was a new prime minister. To all of us, the words 'prime minister' had come to mean Winston Churchill – but that had changed. There'd been a general election straight after Hitler's defeat and Clement Attlee, the Labour leader, was prime minister now. And, it seemed, with a huge majority.*
>
> *We hadn't expected that – not just after Churchill had led Britain to victory in Europe against such odds.'*

There had been no British election throughout the war in Europe: the two main parties had formed a coalition, so that they could focus on winning the war. Then, with Germany beaten, it had been back to party politics and 'business as usual'.

The newspaper – printed before the Japanese surrender – included hardly any reference at all to the fact that there were hundreds of thousands of Allied soldiers still fighting or held as prisoners of war in the Far East.

It all confirmed what the prisoners had known already: for most people in Britain, the war in Europe had been the *only* war.

◆

A jeep drew up outside the camp, and a white woman – the first the prisoners had seen for years – emerged from it. She had come to speak to the men and offer them words of sympathy and support. She was Lady Edwina Mountbatten.

The following day they received a visit from her husband, Lord Louis Mountbatten – Supreme Allied Commander, South East Asia Command; and then a third and final visit, this time from General (soon to be Field Marshal) William Slim.

General Slim (or 'General Not-As-Slim-As-Us-Lot', as one underfed prisoner quipped) had commanded the Fourteenth Army – the Allied forces in Burma. Theirs had been one of the longest and hardest-fought campaigns of the war.

They too had been overlooked: most people in Britain barely knew they existed. As the hugely popular Slim – 'Uncle Bill' to his troops – was said to have told his men:

> When you go home, don't worry about what to tell your loved ones and friends about service in Asia. No one will know where you were, or where it is if you do.
>
> You are, and will remain, the Forgotten Army.

♦

Then, at last, it began.

Every few days, trucks would arrive at Pratchai and a group of prisoners would embark on their long journey home.

Ben was going to have to wait. His job now was to co-ordinate these final stages and ensure that every other prisoner had left the camp by the time that he did. He would be in the last contingent to leave.

He oversaw the evacuation process and decided who should be included in the next batch to go; men's specific circumstances were taken into account, and the sick ones were evenly distributed among the separate departure groups so that they were always travelling with enough others for the fitter men to be able to assist them.

In the meantime, there was no postal service enabling Ben to send a letter home from Pratchai:

> *'So, in each departing group, I would ask a few of my friends who were leaving to write to my mother as soon as they could. I gave them her address.*
>
> *Just to tell her that I was well, and that I was safe, and that I'd be home.'*

Part Six

Back to the Unknown

'The Allies rebuilt Japan and Germany and Italy. Nobody rebuilt our lives. The tears and nightmares will remain till death.'

Jack Edwards
Former prisoner of the Japanese

48

Have You Seen Him?

TOWARDS the end of September, a letter arrived in Edgware addressed to Ben's mother. It was from a man who said that he knew her son, and that Ben was well and would soon be home. It was an immense relief after years of worry.

She received two very similar letters the following day, and several more the day after that; this continued for some time. The initial euphoria began to fade:

'She couldn't understand why she was getting all these messages from people she didn't know, but none from me.

Looking back, I wish I'd written a letter while I was at Pratchai and given it to a friend leaving the camp to post to her as soon as he could. All she knew now was that lots of people who had been with me were back home, but that I wasn't.'

As more and more of the former prisoners returned, further shocking reports of what had happened appeared in the press.

She knew that there were many being kept back at military hospitals in Asia as being unfit to continue their journey home. She had also read about the activities of the Kempeitai. Over time, the letters assuring her that Ben would soon be back – with still no word from him – started to feel like a desperate attempt to shield her from some grim truth.

She was in touch with other parents of men who had been in the Far East: by now, their sons were either home or officially confirmed dead. (Mrs Youle's son, Second Lieutenant Youle from Edgware, was in the second category.)

Then, at last, good news: a telegram from Ben. He was in Colombo in Ceylon, where his ship home had docked; he had not had access to any kind of a postal service until now. He was, he said, travelling on HMS *Chitral* which would be resuming its journey to Southampton soon.

With mounting excitement, the family traced the progress of the *Chitral* each day: west from Ceylon through the Arabian Sea, north through the Red Sea and the Suez Canal, and into the Mediterranean; then past Gibraltar and north through the Bay of Biscay towards Southampton.

Ben's mother, his brothers and sisters and their husbands and wives travelled to Southampton by car. There they were shown into an army camp, where they were directed into a hut set aside for waiting relatives.

Ben's sister Lucy wandered outside the hut, as the newly disembarked soldiers started to appear on the camp. In the late October twilight, the lanky arrivals were hard to tell apart – but, in spite of that, Lucy's gaze immediately fell on one gaunt-faced man in particular. He was so thin that he walked with his arms tucked inside his coat, leaving both his sleeves hanging empty as if he had suffered some dreadful injury; as he came closer, his face began to look so hollow that she feared he had lost all his teeth. But there was no mistaking Ben: she ran up to her long-gone brother, flung her arms around him, and dragged him over to the hut where the rest of the family were waiting.

They were shocked by his appearance – even though they had braced themselves for the worst – and he too was struck by the obvious toll that four exceptionally difficult years had taken on them. His mother had clearly suffered the most.

Yet it was an indescribably happy reunion, and particularly so for Ben. He had not expected his family to be there, and two of them – a new brother-in-law and a new sister-in-law – were people he had never met or even heard of until now.

They spoke until it grew late and relatives were asked to return home. The soldiers were to stay on the camp overnight.

The next morning, the men had some basic medical checks to confirm that they were fit to continue their journeys.

They had been better fed over the past eleven weeks, and particularly so during the long voyage back to Britain. Yet, even after regaining much of his lost weight, Ben – a man of average height – still weighed less than seven stone.

After lunch, the men went their separate ways.

Ben boarded the train for Waterloo and headed out towards a different, unknown version of the world that he remembered; he had only the scantiest knowledge of what had happened during the war that had torn him away.

He saw from his carriage the devastation that the German bombers had inflicted on Southampton. Then, as the train moved further out, the view changed and he saw again the green English countryside that he had missed so much.

◆

It had been a long journey – and a long wait. He had been among the last to leave Pratchai but, eventually, the army trucks to collect the final batch of prisoners had arrived and had taken them to Bangkok. There they had slept for five nights on the floor at the university.

They were in Bangkok for the Jewish Day of Atonement (or *Yom Kippur*), having narrowly missed the Jewish New Year. He and a small number of other Jewish soldiers attended services there and had a meal at the end of the festival with a community of seventy Jewish refugees from Germany.

These were people who had escaped to Bangkok before the outbreak of war. They had been well treated by the Japanese:

'The Japanese just saw them as Germans – their allies!'

The next stage was an afternoon flight to Rangoon in Burma, where the released prisoners spent five days at the military hospital to ensure that they would be fit for the voyage back.

'Not everyone was well enough, unfortunately.

I remember that one of our very best officers – his name was Captain Hughes – died there in the hospital at Rangoon. He'd been with us since the early days at Saigon and had always stood up for his men, time after time.

He'd gone through it all, just to die at the last moment.'

From Rangoon, they had boarded HMS *Chitral* bound for Southampton.

♦

It was evening when the train pulled into Waterloo.

As he stepped onto the platform, Ben's excitement at being back in London was tempered by a stark reminder of what he knew already:

'As we came off the train, we saw people – parents, brothers, sisters – standing at the station, holding up placards.

Each placard had a blown-up photograph of a young man, with a name and a regiment number. The people didn't look at all hopeful, but they stood there with their placards anyway. A lot of them displayed the message:

"HAVE YOU SEEN HIM?"'

It was 29 October 1945 and Ben was among the last to arrive home. Those who had waited and worried and still not heard from their sons, brothers, husbands or fathers knew by now that there was little chance of a happy homecoming; yet, each time a train came in carrying returning soldiers, they turned up with their placards in desperate search of news.

♦

Ben's three brothers were at the station to meet him.

He climbed into the car with them and looked out of the window as they set off from Waterloo:

'More bomb damage – but there was something else too: London was lit up in the dark. I hadn't seen that in ages. No more blackout.'

They headed out of central London towards the northern outskirts of the city. Night had fallen, but everywhere was still recognisable after all this time.

They continued north into Edgware.

It looked just the same as he had remembered it. He had last been here four Jewish New Years ago while stationed at Devonport, having been earmarked for the 'technical instructors' radar course. He had been back at the barracks in the small hours of the following morning, to be told that there had been a change of plan: he was to go overseas in five days' time. There were dark whisperings of Singapore.

They turned into a street where one of the houses was brightly lit and adorned at the front with a huge 'Welcome Back' decking. A sea of faces from the old days had gathered outside to meet him. He was home.

49

Is It True?

ON FRIDAY 13 FEBRUARY 1942 – two days before the fall
of Singapore – Mrs Youle had been at home in Edgware when a
picture of her son had unaccountably fallen onto the floor. It had
happened close to four o'clock in the afternoon.

She knew from that moment, without the slightest hint of a
doubt, that he was dead.

Ben's mother spent many hours over the years that followed
urging Mrs Youle to dismiss that thought from her mind, to see
it as being based on nothing more than superstition and never to
give up hope. But trying to lift her spirits became even more
hopeless as the war dragged on and Mrs Youle heard nothing
from her son – not even one of the three or four standard
postcards that other parents had.

Then the war ended, and Mrs Youle received formal
notification from the War Office. She had been right all along.

On the morning following Ben's return, his mother told him of
her friendship with Mrs Youle and of what had happened.

Ben was astonished to hear the date and time when Second
Lieutenant Youle's photograph had fallen down. Not only was it
the very date – Black Friday – when that bomb had killed Youle
and eight other men; it was also (disregarding regional time
differences) the same time of day.

Ben's mother told him that Mrs Youle had been officially
notified now of the terrible news, but that she knew no details
and wanted to speak to Ben.

'I went along to her house. She told me about the picture falling down, just as my mother had described it to me.

Then she asked for more information, and so I told her what had happened – that a bomb had fallen straight into his gun pit and that he had died instantly.

She took it as bravely as any mother ever could.'

Mrs Youle asked Ben where her son was buried. He drew her a map, showing the front lawn of the Seamen's Mission and the area in the corner of it where they had dug a communal grave for the nine men that dreadful night.

At Ben's suggestion, she took the map to the War Office. The nine bodies were later exhumed and reburied alongside other Allied casualties in the Kranji War Cemetery at Singapore.

♦

Ben returned to his mother's house, where there were visitors waiting to see him. Their questions – which he was to hear incessantly over the days ahead – almost all seemed to start with the words 'Is it true?'

Was it true what they had heard on the radio? Was it true what they had read in the newspapers? Was it true what had been said in the House of Commons?

Visitors left, but not until new ones had arrived, and the final visitors of the day did not leave until around midnight. More came at eight the following morning, and it again went on until midnight – and the same the next day and the day after that.

Ben found that he was answering 'Is it true?' questions sixteen hours a day.

After two continuous weeks of this, he could stand no more. He went to stay in Bournemouth with his sister Lucy and her husband for a short holiday – determined to tell nobody where he had spent the past four years.

It did not work. His abnormal thinness gave him away, and soon he was being approached by other guests and hotel staff and quizzed about his experiences all over again.

'Then, towards the end of my stay, one of the proprietor's daughters came up to me.

She told me they'd arranged a luxury dessert for me that evening, to celebrate my safe return.'

They certainly had. He discovered at dinner that the hotel had gone to extraordinary lengths to obtain ingredients which were exceedingly scarce in post-war Britain, and which could only be obtained at very considerable expense from overseas.

It was, they proudly announced, a special treat: rice pudding.

♦

Ben returned to work at the beginning of 1946.

The following month, four years after his victory at Singapore, General Tomoyuki Yamashita was executed for war atrocities committed both there and in the Philippines.

♦

Five years later, Ben received his call-up papers – again.

This time it was the Korean War. After demobilisation, Ben's name had been placed on a reserve list; on the strength of his radar experience, he had now been selected to fight with the United Nations forces intervening on the side of South Korea.

He reported to the main Royal Artillery barracks at Woolwich, where it quickly became obvious that (owing to his capture at Singapore) his radar knowledge was ten years out of date. It was decided that he should stay for the fifteen-day refresher course but could then consider himself absolved.

Ben could not bring himself to tell his mother where he had spent those fifteen days: the war had taken a terrible toll on her, and the slightest possibility that he could again be posted overseas had not crossed her mind. So he pretended that he had been working at a client's office in Cardiff – a fiction which was maintained for the remaining seven years of her life.

– 50 –
Sixty Years

THE SEVEN HUNDRED MEN who had left Saigon for Thailand were considered – as I have said – to be the fittest two-thirds of the Saigon prisoners.

Almost a third of these seven hundred never returned. Of those who did, many died much younger than they should have done (in some cases soon after arriving home), and many more were plagued by trauma and disability for the rest of their lives.

Adapting to normality was difficult for practically all of them. Some struggled desperately to make others understand the horrors of what they had been through, while others could not speak of it at all. Long-term anxiety and depression – and all the other psychological difficulties that are associated with them – blighted countless lives, and most suffered from nightmares which never left them.

Ordinary personal and working relationships became impossible. Men with families found that they had lost any kind of connection with them, and many were haunted by appalling images that drove them apart from everyone.

The resettlement advice offices could not begin to help with this kind of emotional scarring: the men were expected to return to the demands of normal life, and simply pick up where they had left off.

But many successfully re-adjusted and went on to live long and worthwhile lives. Ben, although he suffered bouts of malaria for more than a decade after his return, was among these.

Several criteria have been identified as determining why re-adjustment was harder for some than for others: the prisoner's age at the time of captivity; the nature of his experiences; the strength of the friendships he made as a prisoner; the level of continuing contact with former comrades after the war; and the nature of the family and other support systems to which he returned when he came home.

The role of religion is less clear-cut. For many, the belief in any kind of a God became impossible and was never restored; some of these adapted well in the years that followed and lived to a good age. The presence or absence of religious faith cannot therefore be cited as a conclusive factor.

Yet there is no doubt that many held on to their beliefs, and found that they drew strength from them during their darkest days. Ben – although he was not naturally given to discussing such matters – felt that this probably applied to him.

After the war, the observant Jewish environment in which he had been brought up remained a central part of his life.

When Ben arrived home, the local synagogue had become too small to accommodate Edgware's Jewish community. Ben headed the project to build new premises: a long and labour-intensive process which involved countless fundraising activities, fraught negotiations with planning authorities and so on.

It took sixteen years, at the end of which the new building was opened with the largest seating capacity at that time of any synagogue in Europe, and the second largest worldwide.

He went on to serve for twenty-four years as an honorary officer of the United Synagogue[18], where he was central to the establishment of two of Britain's main Jewish cemeteries.

♦

---

[18]   This is not a synagogue at all but a statutory organisation constituting the largest mainstream Jewish denominational grouping in Britain.

But I digress: this is a book about Far East prisoners of war.

The peace treaty with Japan required that Japanese assets which had been frozen in Allied and neutral countries at the start of the war be distributed among former prisoners of war and civilian internees. This produced derisory payments of £76 and £49 to each of the prisoners and internees respectively – in return for which all future individual claims were waived.

General Percival, who had led the campaigns at Malaya and Singapore, invited a small group of people to act as an informal committee for the collection and distribution of the assets. One of these was Ben.

Ben – still only a lance-bombardier at the end of the war – had never previously met General Percival or had any other kind of contact with him; he had no idea who had given Percival his name and never found out.

Later the Ministry of Pensions contacted the committee to say that there were some further 'sweepings', and suggested that these be distributed equally among those concerned. However, this would only have produced a payment in the region of five pounds per person. It was becoming increasingly clear that some were in far greater need than others, that their difficulties would continue for many years to come, and that five pounds would not begin to address their problems.

The committee suggested instead that the remaining money be placed in a trust fund, where it could be invested and applied over time for those with the greatest needs.

The government instructed its own lawyers to draw up a trust deed with that in mind. On reviewing the draft deed, Ben identified two main difficulties: insufficient investment powers, and wording which would unintentionally have barred the trust from the valuable tax exemptions available to charities. Both points were corrected, and the deed was finalised.

General Percival asked Ben to be a founder trustee of the fund. This made Ben one of the four former army trustees; the other two (in addition to the general, as chairman) were Air Vice-Marshal Sir Paul Maltby (who had also served as a prisoner of the Japanese) and Brigadier Sir Philip Toosey (of whom more in a moment). There were also three government-appointed trustees: Fred Peart MP (later Lord Peart), Sir Thomas Yates and Brigadier Sir John Smyth VC MC MP.

General Percival devoted the rest of his life to the welfare of former Far East prisoners of war, and also to the International Red Cross, until his death in 1966. After that, he was succeeded as chairman of the trustees by Brigadier Toosey.

As a lieutenant-colonel, Toosey had been an Allied commanding officer on the railway. He has often been spoken of as the real-life version of the Colonel Nicholson character played by Alec Guinness in *The Bridge on the River Kwai*.

However, the film (like the book) is a work of fiction, and particularly so the Nicholson character. Colonel Nicholson is a collaborator, because he goes out of his way to expedite the building of the bridge when he does not need to. Toosey's role was entirely different: he knew the bridge had to be built, and that refusal would be punished by mass execution; having accepted this, his overriding concern was to see that the project would result in the least possible loss of Allied lives.

Far from wishing to see the bridge built to perfection (as in the film), Toosey actively encouraged delay and sabotage: the concrete was badly mixed and white ants and termites were amassed to eat into the wood[19]. He also displayed enormous courage in other respects, persistently standing up to the Japanese and taking repeated beatings from them.

Toosey could easily have avoided all this. His earlier courage during the defence of Singapore – which earned him the Distinguished Service Order – had led to Toosey being ordered to leave the island three days before the surrender, on account of his exceptional leadership qualities; he refused, preferring to remain with his men during their captivity. He became one of the most respected commanders on the railway.

---

[19]   In fact there were two bridges. The main bridge was steel (not wood, as shown in the film), but a temporary wooden bridge had to be built too.

When Toosey died in 1975, Ben, who had acted as his deputy on the trustee board for several years, succeeded him as chairman. It was a role in which Ben would continue until near the end of his life.

With an initial pool equating to roughly five pounds for each former prisoner and internee, the trust had opened with very limited resources. These were supplemented by the proceeds of successful appeals for donations over the years that followed, which were used for former prisoners, internees and their families. Although the trust fund had been established by the UK government, it received no money from the taxpayer[20] and certainly nothing further from the Japanese government.[21]

In 2005, Ben received a formal certificate from the National Federation of Far East Prisoners of War Clubs and Associations:

> This Certificate of Appreciation is in grateful recognition by the Federation of 50 years of dedicated service, of which 29 years have been as Chairman of the Far East (Prisoners of War and Internees) Fund and Far East Prisoner of War Central Welfare Fund. Furthermore it is in recognition of expertise in the management of these Funds thus enabling assistance to many ex-Far East prisoners of war in times of need and stress.

He continued this work for a further two years, after which his worsening eyesight finally made it necessary for him to stand down. He was ninety-one.

♦

---

[20] The British government did however eventually provide former prisoners with a one-off 'special gratuity' of £10,000 per head in late 2000, after more than half a century of campaigning. Being fifty-five years after the end of the war, this was too late for a great many of those who had suffered.

[21] Those who were to blame for these events resolutely refused to acknowledge or display any kind of remorse for Japan's wartime past; it was left to a later generation of Japanese to express the first glimmerings of formal apologies for what had happened, more than fifty years after the end of the war – but still there has never been any meaningful offer of compensation.

This was never supposed to be a book about Ben's entire life.

I have said practically nothing, for example, about his early years in London's East End – in the aftermath of the Great War, and then under the storm clouds of the Great Depression.

I have not told about Ben's experience of being struck with a police baton at the 'Battle of Cable Street', where hundreds of thousands of anti-fascist protesters successfully prevented the British Union of Fascists from marching through Jewish areas of East London. Nor have I tried to convey the horrors of living in London during the Blitz.

And I have not described – because I cannot begin to imagine it for myself – the shock after coming home of learning the full abominable truth about the Nazi holocaust.

Instead, this book is specifically about one man's journey through four momentous years.

What happened during that time was unforgettable, but it was not those events or anything else I have mentioned in this book that mattered to him most. The dominant themes of his post-war life were more mundane: the happiness of his marriage to my mother, the responsibilities of supporting a family, and the challenges of bringing up children in a rapidly changing world.

My father – I have finished calling him Ben – died on 12 March 2009, still wearing the gold signet ring that he had kept hidden in his army shaving brush for over three years.

He was almost ninety-three. More than sixty years had elapsed since his return home, and more than seventeen years had passed since my conversations with him which have formed the basis of this book.

There is something further, however, that needs to be said. It is not much, but the book would be incomplete without it.

I shall put it into a separate afterword.

Afterword

THE TAPED INTERVIEWS with my father on which this book is based were recorded fifty years after the catastrophic campaigns at Malaya and Singapore.

There were some memories that he mentioned to me in between recordings, but which he did not talk about with the tapes running. I shall refer to only two of them here.

The first was the occasional arrival at the camps of 'comfort women' – a revolting euphemism for women and girls who had been abducted from their homes in the Japanese-occupied territories, and coerced into lives of forced prostitution.

They were brought to the camps as sex slaves, for the benefit of the guards. He said relatively little about this subject, although his abhorrence – and sadness – at this treatment of people was obvious.

The second of these recollections concerned the screaming that would be heard on the camp during leg amputations. (You will recall that there were no anaesthetics then at Kinsayok.)

That second point is not new: it is self-evident from what I have already said about the amputations. But it is only here that I have spelt it out.

Most of this book should be seen in that way.

For example, he told me about the prisoners' illnesses in mainly factual terms; he did not describe the raw emotional impact of seeing his friends suffer and die in such desolate surroundings (and I would not have expected or wanted him to).

The same applies to the gnawing hunger, the open-ditch latrines, the Kempeitai, the burials, the beatings and the cholera: he told me the facts, but left me to imagine for myself the daily horror, humiliation, and crushing sense of hopelessness of living in that world.

I have tried to carry that same approach into this book.

◆

Finally, one last point – but an important one.

I have recently learned of a number of sickening atrocities (not recounted here) which took place at Kinsayok during the *Speedo* – not only at the main camp, but also at the jungle camp during the fifteen days that he spent there.

He must certainly have known about these incidents at the time (and, I have no doubt, other incidents too). He presumably would have seen them.

Yet he never spoke of them – or not, at least, to me.

Some memories, I am sure, died with him.

Appendix

'My Experiences as a Prisoner of War in Thailand'

Appendix

'My Experiences as a Prisoner of War in Thailand'

THE FOLLOWING PAGES set out my father's essay, referred to in Chapter 32. It was written by order of the Japanese, less than six months after completion of the railway.

He was one of several prisoners required by the Japanese to produce accounts of their experiences for radio broadcast, to counteract recent bad publicity. For obvious reasons, the essay was not used.

The latter part of it refers to some improvements made on the camp following the completion of the railway. These were attributable to a combination of three causes: a conscious effort by the Japanese to improve their standing following international criticism of their conduct towards prisoners; a more relaxed attitude among the Japanese commandant and guards as a result of the early completion of the line;[22] and the strength of personality of the Allied medical officers (particularly 'Weary' Dunlop) in pressing for changes.

However, the prisoners did not know at that time that the Japanese were withholding Red Cross parcels of clothing, food and essential medicines – or that men would be sent out on dangerous work again within weeks. Nor could they know that official Japanese policy towards them would reach its deadliest level yet[23] within a matter of months.

---

[22] It is understood that the Japanese at Kinsayok received some special recognition for the fact that the railway work in their area had been finished in particularly good time – due of course to the ferocity of the *Speedo* there.

[23] Chapter 45.

MY EXPERIENCES
AS A PRISONER OF WAR IN THAILAND

We left Saigon on the 22nd of June 1943 having spent 15 months there. Our party consisted of 700 reasonably fit British POWs.

We travelled from Saigon to Phnom Penh in three small river boats, there being 250 on each of two and 200 on the third. The boat on which I travelled had 250 POWs aboard in addition to the Japanese guard in charge of us and the Annamite crew.

The boat, according to the licence exhibited, was authorised to carry a maximum of 100 passengers. Needless to say we were terribly overcrowded and, as we took 48 hours instead of the usual 24 hours, we had a rather uncomfortable journey with short rations.

From Phnom Penh to Bangkok we travelled by rail, there being approximately 60 to a large goods truck and 30 in the smaller ones. From Bangkok we proceeded in the same trucks to Nong Pladuk. We were furnished with two small hot meals during this train journey which lasted roughly 36 hours, one at Battambang and the other at Bangkok.

We spent three days at Nong Pladuk pending arrangements being made for the rest of the journey and we welcomed the rest after the weary travelling. We left Nong Pladuk on *the 29th June 1943 at 0030 hours and marched in darkness to Ban Pong where we boarded sideless bogey trucks which were loaded with rails and sleepers. We had to perch ourselves on these as best we could – about 40 to a truck. There was no sleep for us for fear of falling off and before long we felt extremely cramped. At Kanburi where the train stopped for half an hour each man was issued with a small rissole. We saw a POW Cemetery en route.*

We arrived at Tarsao Station at about 6.30 p.m. and we then marched to the camp along a very poor road which was very muddy and rather slippery. At Tarsao Camp we met several friends who were in hospital[24], and whom we had not seen for 15 months. We were shocked to learn of the deaths in Thailand of numerous friends whom we had left at Changi in perfect health. Everybody we saw at Tarsao was surprised at and commented on the good condition of our clothes and health. They would have been dismayed if they could have seen us a month later!

At Tarsao Cemetery we saw a POW funeral as we were going to the hut where we were to spend the night. It was here that we first came into contact with cholera.
Many of us went without food that evening as there was insufficient to feed the party and it was not considered worth the trouble of making another journey in the dark and wet to the cookhouse which was situated over a mile away.

---

[24] References to 'hospitals' here simply mean sick huts.

Our breakfast the following morning consisted of rice and tea, and at about 9 a.m. we crammed into barges containing stores etc. in parties of 60 to a barge.

We arrived at No. 2 Jungle Camp[25], Kinsayok at about 9 p.m. that evening. It was raining and there was no accommodation for us – so we had to remain in the barges overnight. The two bargees took about a quarter of the space for themselves and we had to push into the remaining room. Once again, no sleep that night.

An improvised meal proved to be totally unpalatable and few had more than half a pint of tea. We were, after a week of travelling under conditions with little sleep and food, beginning to feel weary.

We were given the following day, 1st July 1943, to get fixed up. we had had no previous experience of jungle camp life and we were faced with the task of having to clear the jungle for a site, cut bamboo and fell trees for staging on which to sleep, unload our tents from the barges, build a cookhouse, dig a deep latrine, erect a fence around the camp, cut a flight of steps in the bank leading down to the river, collect rations, water and firewood for the cookhouse, etc.

---

[25] This is the camp that I simply call 'Kinsayok Jungle Camp'. It was referred to as 'No. 2' camp at the time, to distinguish it from other numbered jungle camps (separate from Kinsayok Main Camp), which are referred to later on.

We worked very hard and got the essential jobs done, but the camp was far from complete by the following morning when we started on the track.

A 'Speedo' of one month's duration started at the same time, due to the work being behind schedule.

We worked for 15 days on the line whilst we were in camp and our work entailed a walk of between 3 and 4 kilometres each way. The work consisted of building embankments with the earth which we dug from the sides or with rocks which we dislodged from the mountainside by drilling holes with hammer and chisel for the explosives to be inserted and set off. The debris we shifted was either used for building the embankments or was carried away.

We also built five wooden bridges across ravines. This entailed the carrying out of the newly felled timber from the jungle to the sites of the bridges and hauling them into position either manually or by the aid of hand-operated winches. This was particularly heavy work as the timber was green and the jungle undergrowth and the inclines hindered our passage.

On the morning of the 17th July 1943 at about 9 a.m. a party of 500 of us marched to the main camp at Kinsayok, where I am stationed at present. On arrival at about 6 p.m. we were given a meal following which we had to fix up our camp once again. We started work again the following morning.

The work consisted of building a very big bridge on an embankment which we made. We felled the majority of the timber and had to carry nearly the whole of it out of the jungle.

Two elephants were used to help occasionally, but strange to relate these beasts were given the smallest timbers to drag whilst we were allotted the heaviest. We had to carry some very heavy timbers from this camp to the site of the bridge some 3 kilometres away and we were not allowed to drop our load for a few minutes' breather. We also worked on making a very big cutting.

Our days, both here and at the jungle camp, commenced at about 6 a.m. when we got up to get our breakfast. We were on parade shortly after 7 a.m. and it was not long before we moved off on our way to work – with just the first signs of daybreak appearing.

We worked until at least 8 p.m. and quite often as late as 10 p.m. with only a break of about 15 minutes in the morning and the same in the afternoon. We stopped for our midday meal, which we barely had time to gulp down before assembling for the afternoon's work.

It was generally midnight or later by the time we got to bed, due to having to get one's evening meal, attend roll-call, have a bath in the river and boil some water to take to work with us the following day.

The food we were getting was insufficient and of poor quality, our meals being as follows:

Breakfast: *Rice, ½ pint of thin stew and ½ pint of tea;*

Tiffin: *Rice, dried fish and ½ pint of boiled water, or, if available, tea;*

Evening: *Rice, ½ pint of thin stew, ½ pint of tea and occasionally a rissole with little taste.*

Many men were injured in the course of the 'Speedo' work, some being quite accidental whilst others should never have occurred. For example, men were made to continue their work at the foot of the slopes whilst others were prising down heavy boulders from off those slopes. It was inevitable that the men would get hurt working under these conditions and many had boulders crash down on them. Refusal to work under these terrible circumstances – as also the keeping of a watchful eye on the falling boulders – resulted in severe corporal punishment.

There was never any attempt at picking men of the same height for the carrying of timbers. Men of all heights were chosen by the engineers. Thus, for example, a log which required twelve men was given to the first twelve available men, and when it was seen that four were not taking any weight due to being short, they were withdrawn – leaving the eight to strain themselves to a degree of exhaustion. Further they were beaten if, as a result of this, they were not moving fast enough to please the engineer in charge.

We used to meet for our midday meal whilst we were stationed at No. 2 Jungle Camp at a little clearing near No. 3 Jungle Camp. There was no shelter here from the rain which was always heavy during our break. The clearing was too near to the scene of blasting as there were often lumps of stone hurtled into our midst. On one occasion two men were badly cut by these flying missiles and had to be taken back to camp.

A very unpleasant feature of our work was the frequency with which men were beaten for no reason. As an example, men suffered in this way for not understanding what was said to them in Japanese. The beatings were administered by open hand, clenched fist, bamboo stick, pick helves, augers, boot kicks, throwing of stones, etc. etc. Life was at times unbearable on account of these undeserved punishments that were meted out.

Many of our men fell sick with dysentery at No. 2 Jungle Camp – due no doubt to the bad sanitation, and lack of sterilisers. We were not permitted to have any men remain in camp to look after these jobs. These sick men were made to go to work in spite of the medical officer's protests that they were passing blood and mucus and were totally unfit.

We have lost many lives that might have been saved if the opinions of the medical officers had been respected. Many others who had bad ulcers were made to go to work and of these several have since had their legs amputated.

In due course, after the completion of the line in our sector, our sick were evacuated downriver and we were disgusted to see that their boots were taken from them on the grounds that sick men did not require any. The boots were taken off evacuee officers despite the fact that they were subject to a general stoppage of pay for clothing, whether supplied or not.

My sojourn as a POW in Thailand can be regarded as covering two distinct periods, namely:-

(1)   the period during which the POWs were building the railway between Ban Pong and Moulmein, and

(2)   the period subsequent thereto.

The reason for differentiating between these periods is that our treatment, conditions and experiences were very much worse in the first than in the second.

It is no exaggeration to say that we were subjected, during the building of the line, to such terrible hardships, trials, exertions, sickness, degradation and misery as few have ever experienced or been called on to endure. It is to be questioned whether there was ever a blacker era in the annals of prisoner-of-war captivity than the one through which we passed during the time in question.

To deal with the conditions under which we lived in greater detail, I make the following observations:-

(1)   FOOD

Our diet has been seriously unbalanced and deficient in many ways. We have missed the qualitative goodness in the food which is essential to good health. The deficiencies in certain vitamins, fats, etc. have led to many types of illnesses as for example, Beri-Beri, ulcers, failing eyesight, skin diseases, etc.

(2)   ACCOMMODATION

During the rainy season of 1943 – whilst the line was in course of construction – large numbers of men were quartered and overcrowded in leaking, unserviceable tentage. The men returned to camp from work in a soaking condition and had to sleep in these wet tents, with only wet bed clothes to cover them. The spreading of infection and disease as a result of the overcrowding was always a great danger. The position nowadays is very much better as a result of the erection of the existing huts.

(3)   WORK

We struck a very bad patch when we first arrived. We were inexperienced in the sort of work that was entailed in the rail-road project. Our arrival coincided with the institution in our sector of a month's 'Speedo'. We worked very long hours and were overworked to the point of exhaustion.

Sick men were forced to go out to work when they should have been nursed. Many cases of our men being badly beaten took place for little or no reason. We were made to suffer because – through no fault of our own – the work on the line was behind schedule.

The effects could be seen at the end of the month's 'Speedo', when out of our party of 700 relatively fit men the Japanese authorities on examining us very minutely could only pronounce 197 (of whom 20 had been cooks and had not worked on the line) as fit enough to go up-country to do some further work on the railway. At this time our medical officer was badly beaten for having so many sick in the battalion.

During August and September 1943, of the people who stayed behind at Kinsayok, only a quarter of them were fit to do extremely light work. These facts must surely speak for themselves. It must be stated that the work since the completion of the line has been very much easier.

(4)   HEALTH

The health of POWs has been lamentably poor, due to the heavy work and lack of goodness in the food. Illnesses have not received the attention they required owing to the gross shortage of medical supplies. Hence the alarming number of deaths.

In my own battalion we have suffered to date 106 deaths out of the 700 men that came to Thailand 8 months ago, namely a death rate of almost 23% per annum.[26] In our previous P.O.W. camp where we were stationed for 15 months, we lost 27 through illness out of the 1,123[27] there, namely a death rate of not quite 2% per annum. Is it necessary to comment on the comparison afforded by these figures, except to say that they certainly show the effects of the manner in which we were worked as briefly mentioned above? I am led to believe that our losses were not particularly heavier than those sustained by other battalions on the river.

Before leaving this question, it must be noted that, since the completion of the line, the Japanese authorities in this camp have done much to cut

---

[26]   The eventual death rate rose above the level stated here, and is likely already to have done so by the time that this was written. This is because some of the sick prisoners who had been moved to other camps such as Tarsao and Chungkai would almost certainly have died by this time.

[27]   In the book, I say a thousand. Page xiii (under the heading *The 'Hanoi Hundred'*) explains the discrepancy.

down illnesses. Thus the Sanitation Squad has built new hygienic latrines and swill-pits in place of the old ones which were breeding places for all sorts of disease carriers. A new hospital[28] was built and an organised drive against rats was encouraged. We have also been inoculated several times against cholera, typhus and plague.[29]

(5) RATES OF PAY

Owing to the low purchasing power of the local currency particularly in this area, our pay does not go very far. Without going into great details it will be appreciated that after stoppages for buying extra rations for the cookhouses and hospital, we can but buy a very small quantity of tobacco and the rest goes on extra food in the form of eggs, sugar, bananas, etc. whenever available.

(6) CLOTHING

We who first came to Thailand reasonably well clad were shocked to see the bad condition of the clothing of those who had arrived before us. Large numbers were wearing only loincloths. Many were without footwear of any kind, yet they had to walk

---

[28] Again, this means new sick huts – not a hospital in the normal sense of the word. Lack of medicines and other resources remained a problem.

[29] These are the most material improvements of the 'post-railway' era. The context of these changes has been briefly outlined on page 209.

many kilometres over sharp granite chippings which were as treacherous as the slippery, slushy mud paths of the jungle.

(7)   **AMENITIES**

We have missed the normal help which the International Red Cross Society ministers to POWs all over the world. We have experienced the lack of mental exercise and the facilities to pursue serious study. We should like to write home more frequently, preferably by letter in lieu of the stereotyped form issued to us on four occasions during the last two years – and to receive mail more regularly. In my battalion of 700 men only four letters have been received since we were made POWs.

In conclusion I would like to state that the experiences set out above are true as can be verified by those who were in the same position as myself. I have however tried to record them in as dispassionate a manner as is possible.

*The above essay was written
by L/BDR Kandler, R,
on the 4ᵗʰ day of March 1944
by order of the Japanese.*

Bibliography

THE FOLLOWING BOOKS have helped me with the historical background and enabled me to confirm my understanding of the facts wherever possible:

Adams, Geoffrey Pharaoh, *No Time For Geishas*, Corgi, 1974.

Caffrey, Kate, *Out in the Midday Sun: Singapore 1941-45 – The End of an Empire*, Stein and Day, New York, 1973.

Chalker, Jack B., *Burma Railway: Images of War*, Mercer Books, 2007.

Daws, Gavin, *Prisoners of the Japanese: POWs of the Second World War in the Pacific*, Pocket Books, 1994.

Dunlop, E. E., *The War Diaries of Weary Dunlop*, Penguin Books, 1988.

Ebury, Sue, *Weary: The Life of Sir Edward Dunlop*, Penguin Books, 1995.

Hardie, Dr Robert, *The Burma-Siam Railway*, Quadrant, 1983.

Kinvig, Clifford, *River Kwai Railway: The Story of the Burma-Siam Railroad*, Conway, 2005.

MacArthur, Brian, *Surviving the Sword: Prisoners of the Japanese 1942-45*, Time Warner Books, 2005.

Pavillard, Stanley S., *Bamboo Doctor*, Macmillan, 1960.

Smith, Colin, *Singapore Burning: Heroism and Surrender in World War II*, Penguin Books, 2006.

Summers, Julie, *Stranger in the House*, Pocket Books, 2009.

Thompson, Peter, *The Battle for Singapore: The True Story of the Greatest Catastrophe of World War II*, Portrait, 2006.

Urquhart, Alistair, *The Forgotten Highlander*, Little, Brown, 2010.

Warren, Alan, *Britain's Greatest Defeat: Singapore 1942*, Hambledon Continuum, 2007.

Index

AN ASTERISK means that the name shown is a pseudonym:

* denotes a pseudonym.

Further Information

www.ThePrisonerList.com

MANY PEOPLE have asked to see a copy of my father's record book, normally in order to look up a specific name. Because of its nature, I remain uneasy about displaying the book too widely over the internet; however, I can see no harm it making it available to those with a genuine interest.

To view the record book, therefore, the first step is to visit *www.ThePrisonerList.com* and select *Further Research* from the main menu. The first item on that page, headed *The Original Prisoner List*, enables you to request access.

The remainder of that *Further Research* page sets out other leads and internet links which may be helpful to you.

The website contains some other interesting material too, including video clips from the interviews with my father and a short film (appropriately called *The Prisoner List*) made by Kate Owen and Danny Roberts which is based on this book.

◆

Finally, a word of warning: I am an obsessive tinkerer, and so it may well be that the contents or layout of the website will have changed by the time you read this.

You may even find that the site is no longer there. I hope to continue maintaining it for as long as I can, but the future is hard to predict.

Richard Kandler

Lightning Source UK Ltd.
Milton Keynes UK
UKOW04f1503300914

239418UK00001B/22/P